UKRAINIAN CATHOLICS IN AMERICA

A History

Bohdan P. Procko
Villanova University

UNIVERSITY
PRESS OF
AMERICA

BX
4711.72
.P76
1982

To the memory of the pioneers;
For the enrichment of:
Frances, Georgeanne, Paul, Peter, and Rosemary

ACKNOWLEDGMENTS

This book grew out of the writer's doctoral dissertation submitted to the Faculty of Arts at the University of Ottawa, Canada, in 1964. The author wishes to express his appreciation to numerous institutions and individuals for their varied contributions to the work.

Special gratitude is owed to the first Metropolitan of the Ukrainian Catholic Archdiocese of Philadelphia, the Most Reverend Constantine Bohachevsky; to his successor, the late Metropolitan Ambrose Senyshyn; to the former Chancellor, Msgr. Michael Poloway; and to the former Econom, Very Rev. Basil Holowinsky, through whose cooperation the writer made use of the archdiocesan archival materials.

Gratitude is due also to Messrs. Anthony Dragan, former Editor-in-Chief, and the late Bohdan Krawciw, Editor, of Svoboda, Jersey City, N. J.; to Michael Roman, former Editor-in-Chief of the Amerikansky Russky Viestnik, Munhall, Pa. (now called the Greek Catholic Union Messenger); to Michael Pasika, former Editor of America, Philadelphia, Pa.; to John R. Dudish, former Retail Advertising Manager of the Evening Herald, Shenandoah, Pa.; and to the late Oleksa H. Hankewych, Custodian of the archives of the Ukrainian National Museum, Chicago, Ill.

The writer is thankful to Professors Alfred R. Vanasse, the late Constantine Bida, Richard A. LeBrun, all of the University of Ottawa; the late Roman Small-Stocki, of Catholic University of America; and Jerome J. Fischer, of Villanova University. Their advice and critical reading of the manuscript led to changes which have improved this work. Indebtedness is acknowledged, also, to Mrs. Bess Polkowski for typing the entire manuscript, frequently under difficult conditions. Furthermore, I wish to thank the editors of Diakonia, The Catholic Historical Review, Pennsylvania History, The Ukrainian Quarterly, and the Directors of the Associated University Presses, Inc., (copyrighters of The Ethnic Experience in Pennsylvania, ed. by John E. Bodnar) for permission to use portions of my articles which were first printed in their publications.

Lastly, I am immeasurably indebted to my wife, Margaret, without whose sacrifice this study could not have been completed. To all those individuals and institutions, named and unnamed, the author expresses his sincere gratitude.

B.P.P.
Villanova, Pa.

CONTENTS

NOTE ON TRANSLITERATION

The system of transliteration followed is that of
the Library of Congress; except that the letters
є , й , ю , я , when initial letters of words, are trans-
literated as "ye", "y", "yu", "ya"; the letter и and
the final ий and ый are rendered "y"; and all dia-
critical marks are omitted.

As a rule, names of persons, organizations, etc.
are rendered according to the English spelling used by
the individual persons and organizations; in instances
where the names of individuals have to be transliter-
ated by the writer, the first names are given in their
English equivalents and the last names according to
the system stated.

The names of well-known Ukrainian historical
personages and geographical designations follow the
forms generally accepted in English usage, with the
Ukrainian spelling frequently given in parentheses to
avoid possible confusion in the identification. In
instances of less known geographical designations the
Ukrainian spelling is given, and if deemed pertinent
another version is provided in parentheses.

x

LIST OF ABBREVIATIONS

AER	American Ecclesiastical Review (Ecclesiastical Review from 1908 through 1943)
Almanakh Svobody	Yuvyleiny almanakh Svobody, 1893-1953
Almanakh Tserkvy	Yuvyleiny almanakh Ukrainskoi Hreko-Katolytskoi Tserkvy u Zluchenykh Derzhavakh, 1884-1934
AAS	Acta Apostolicae Sedis
ASS	Acta Sanctae Sedis
CD	Catholic Directory
CE	Catholic Encyclopedia
Directory of Races	U. S. Senate. Dictionary of Races or Peoples
ECQ	Eastern Churches Quarterly
HPL	Homiletic and Pastoral Review
Kalendar Sojedinenija	Kalendar Greko Kaftoliceskaho Sojedinenija
Kalendar Soyuza	Kalendar Ukrainskoho Narodnoho Soyuza
Knyha kaledza	Propamiatna knyha ukrainskoho katolytskoho kaledza
Knyha katedry	Propamiatna knyha ukrainskoi katolytskoi katedry
Knyha Soyuza	Propamiatna knyha Ukrainskoho Narodnoho Soyuza, 1894-1934
Pershy kalendar	Pershy rusko-amerykansky kalendar
Shipman Memorial	A Memorial of Andrew J. Shipman (C. B. Pallen, ed.)
St. Michael's Book	St. Michael's Diamond Jubillee Book (Shenandoah)
Tserkva sv. Yura	Piatdesiatlittia Ukrainskoi Katolytskoi Tserkvy sv. Yura
Ukrainian Directory	Directory of the Byzantine Rite Ecclesiastical Province of Philadelphia. Before 1958, Directory of the Apostolic Exarchate of Philadelphia
Ukrainska Mytropolia	Ukrainska Katolytska Mytropolia v Zluchenykh Derzhavakh Ameryky

Ukraintsi u sviti   Ukraintsi u vilnomu sviti:
                           yuvileina knyha Ukrainskoho
                           Narodnoho Soyuza, 1894-1954
Viestnik   Amerikansky Russky Viestnik
Visty   Eparkhiialny Vistnyk,
                           Eparkhiialni Visty from 1924,
                           and Archeparkhiialni Visti
                           from November 1958

INTRODUCTION

Serious economic, social, and political hardships brought large numbers of people from Eastern
Europe, particularly from the Austro-Hungarian Empire,
to the new world in the second half of the nineteenth
century. Most of them came to the United States, thus
introducing new and unfamiliar cultures, traditions,
and languages into American society. Conditions in
Eastern Europe following both World Wars tended to
continue and even expand the migration of peoples.
Consequently, for over a century and a quarter now,
Americans of various Eastern European origins have
been contributing their cultures and customs to the
new world. In America, the customs of the immigrants
from Eastern Europe became intermingled with those of
the West to a greater degree than they ever had been
in Western European society prior to World War II.
One of the cultural traditions that many Americans of
Eastern European origin are most proud of is the
Byzantine-Slavic religious heritage which they brought
with them to the new world.

The religious traditions of Americans of Ukrainian descent were formed in the ninth and tenth centuries. Christianity was briefly introduced into the
territory of present day Ukraine by Byzantine missionaries in the ninth century. In the tenty century
Princess Olga (Olha) of Kiev accepted Eastern Christianity and was baptized in 957. It was Grand Duke
Vladimir (Volodymyr), however, who laid the permanent
foundation of the Byzantine-Slavic religious traditions in the Kievan Principality when he and the
people of Kiev accepted Christianity officially in
988.[1]

It was from the territories of present day
Western Ukraine, at the time under the political control of Austria-Hungary, that the mass Ukrainian immigration to the United States began in the last
quarter of the nineteenth century. Virtually all of
those immigrants were Catholics of the Byzantine-
Slavic rite in communion with Rome.[2] Emigration from
the eastern Ukrainian territories--that part under
Russian political control--was practically impossible;
there were, therefore, almost no representation of the

Ukrainian Orthodox among the early immigrants.

The new immigrants were generally known as Ruthenians, a term the medieval Latin sources usually applied to the western groups of the Eastern Slavs. The name is a Latinization of Slavic <u>Rusyny</u> (Rusini), which is derived from Kievan Rus.[3] Since at least the end of the sixteenth century the term has been used by the Papacy as a common name for "those peoples of the Byzantine rite who inhabited a region of Europe situated roughly between Lithuania in the North and Carpathian mountains in the South."[4]

With the rise of national consciousness in the latter part of the nineteenth and early twentieth centuries the peoples of this region became generally known by national names, such as: Ukrainians, Byelorussians, Rusyns,[5] Carpatho-Russians, and Slovaks. The particular discipline of the Byzantine rite that these people followed continued, however, to be referred to as Ruthenian.[6]

Until the formation in 1916 of separate ecclesiastical administrations for the Ukrainians from Austrian Galicia and Bukovina and for the Rusyns and others from Hungary's Transcarpathia (Subcarpathia), the early history of the Ukrainian Catholic Church in America was largely the common history of the Ukrainian and Rusyn immigrants. Their early parishes, characterized by mixed congregations and presided by priests from different sections of Austria-Hungary, were referred to in official documents as Ruthenian. For clarity, when discussing the development of the Ukrainian Catholic Church prior to 1916 the "umbrella" term Ruthenian will frequently be used to reflect the common religious experiences of immigrants of varied national backgrounds.[7] When their origin is clearcut, the name Ukrainian will be used for the immigrants from Austrian Galicia and Bukovina, while the term Transcarpathian will be employed for those from Hungary.

CHAPTER I

IMMIGRATION, ORGANIZATION, AND CONFLICTS

1. Ruthenian Immigrants

Immigrants designated as Ruthenians began arriving from Austria-Hungary at least as early as the 1860's;[1] mass migration, however, did not start until the late 1870's when agents of Pennsylvania anthracite mining companies succeeded in recruiting workers from Transcarpathia and Slovakia[2] in Hungary for the most menial jobs in and about the mines. Quickly the news spread north to neighboring Lemkivschyna (Lemko Land) in Austria's Galicia.[3] Galician Lemkivschyna was the territory on the northern slopes of the Carpathians, whereas Transcarpathia was the region on the southern slopes of the same mountains.

The first Transcarpathian immigrants, it appears, came from Hungary's northeastern counties of Zemelin, Sarys, Spis, and Aba-Uj. Later they came from Uz, Bereg, Ugocha, Maramorosh, and other localities.[4] They settled primarily in Pennsylvania, later, in lesser numbers, in Minnesota, Colorado, and Montana. They were employed as laborers by the coal, silver, and gold mines, steel mills, saw mills, lumber companies, brick factories, and the railroads.[5] It was from the mountainous border districts of western Galicia that the earliest mass Ukrainian emigration originated. According to Nestor Dmytriw (Dmytrov), a very active Ukrainian priest in immigrant affairs after 1895, the Lemky from Galicia came mostly from Novy Sanch, Horlytsi and Krosno counties. They settled, in groups primarily in Pennsylvania communities like Shenandoah, Shamokin, Mount Carmel, Hazleton, Lansford, Freeland, Olyphant, and Mayfield, and in Jersey City, New Jersey, Yonkers and Troy, New York, and Ansonia and New Britain, Connecticut.[6] Eastern Galicia and Bukovina did not contribute to this immigration until the 1890's,[7] and the Ukrainian immigration from the Russian empire remained relatively insignificant until the First World War.[8] Based on the estimates of an early American expert on Ruthenian immigrant problems, there were close to

1,000 Ruthenians in the anthracite region of Pennsylvania alone in 1880; 20,000 in 1890; and 40,000 in 1900.[9]

The early Ruthenian immigrants were peasants whose economic condition was so hopeless, particularly in Galicia, that the tales of the opportunities in America were sufficient to prompt the more adventurous among them to seek a way out of their predicament.[10] The poverty-stricken peasants who made their way to America were immediately confronted with serious cultural and linguistic problems not faced by earlier immigrants from the countries of western Europe. This proved to be particularly serious since the early Ruthenian immigrants did not have any representation from the educated classes[11] (until the arrival of their priests), a representation that might have made the period of transition less difficult by providing a more qualified leadership. Lacking leadership when it was badly needed, the immigrants often fell prey to unscrupulous agents of one sort or another.[12]

Thrust in unfamiliar and sometimes hostile surroundings, the immigrants felt the need for their own familiar institutions, above all their own church, which had been the center of their social life in Europe. Obviously, until a sufficient number of immigrants had settled in close proximity to one another, serious action towards that end could not be taken. Until the arrival of their own priests and the organization of their own churches, the immigrants attended the Latin rite churches, particularly those of their European neighbors like the Poles, Slovaks, or the Hungarians. Many of those who remained in the Latin churches eventually lost their national identity.

By 1882 there were about sixty to seventy Ruthenian families in Shenandoah, Pennsylvania,[13] and it was these immigrants who in 1884 made the first attempt to obtain a priest from Europe. With the help of Carol Rice, himself an immigrant from Lithuania, the Shenandoah immigrants sent a petition to the Metropolitan of Galicia, the Most Reverend Sylvester Sembratovich, Archbishop of Lviv (Lvov), requesting that a priest be sent to minister to their religious needs.[14] The immigrants had come in contact with Rice at the travel and exchange agency he operated, where they frequently made arrangements for mailing money to their relatives in Europe. From

2

these business relations Rice learned of their religious needs and aspirations. In a letter dated October 24, 1884,[15] Metropolitan Sembratovich (later Cardinal) informed the Shenandoah immigrants that he had appointed the Reverend John Volansky, from the Archdiocese of Lviv, as their missionary pastor. Volansky, a Ukrainian, arrived in Shenandoah on December 10, 1884. As the first Ruthenian priest in the United States, he began the formal organization of the Ruthenian church.[16]

Father Volansky's missionary work was by no means an easy task, and numerous obstacles confronted him, as he indicates in his "Recollections From By-Gone Years".[17] Misunderstandings with the Latin rite hierarchy and clergy were, unfortunately, part of the problems facing him. On his arrival in the United States Father went to Shenandoah to acquaint himself with his people. After this he immediately made a courtesy call on the Archbishop of Philadelphia, the Most Reverend Patrick J. Ryan, who, Volansky states, had already been notified of his coming by the Polish priest in Shenandoah. The Archbishop's Vicar General, Very Rev. Maurice A. Walsh, who received Father Volansky, refused to accept his credentials and forbid him to perform his priestly functions, saying that there was no room for a married priest in America.[18] A comparable reception was also accorded Volansky by the three pastors in Shenandoah. Although it was true, as Father Heuser explained in 1891, that there was never an occasion nor the necessity for the American student of theology to familiarize himself with the usages of the Byzantine rite prior to the arrival of the Ruthenians,[19] it seems that more willingness in the beginning to understand each others problems would have helped to prevent more serious misunderstandings later on.

From Shenandoah Volansky telegraphed Metropolitan Sembratovich informing him of his difficulties and stating that he would begin his priestly functions based on the jurisdiction given him by the Metropolitan. When no prohibitive reply from his superior was forthcoming, Volansky rented a hall on Main street for the purpose of holding religious services.[20] Thus it was in Kern Hall that the first Byzantine rite Catholic service, Vespers, was celebrated on Wednesday evening, December 18, 1884, with young Gregory Dolny serving as Father's first Cantor. The temporary chapel in this hall was dedicated to the Immaculate

3

Conception of the Blessed Virgin Mary.[21]

Early in 1885 the parishioners elected a committee to take charge of the church building program.
To finance the project each family was assessed ten
dollars plus one dollar monthly dues, whereas single
persons were expected to contribute half that amount.
Subsequently two lots were purchased on the north side
of Center Street for $700.00, and the construction of
the church began in the Spring. Before the building
was completed the roof collapsed, due to structural
imperfections, making extensive rebuilding necessary,
delaying completion of the church until the fall of
1886, and raising the total cost to above $20,000. On
November 21, 1886, this first Byzantine-Slavic rite
Catholic Church in the United States, dedicated to St.
Michael the Archangel, was blessed by its pastor, Rev.
John Volansky.

Father Volansky's missionary work was not limited
to Shenandoah alone. Within weeks after his arrival
in Shenandoah, Volansky was attending to the spiritual
needs of immigrants living in near-by communities,
such as those in the Shamokin area. Although a great
number of the immigrants settled in the coal regions
of Pennsylvania, a substantial number were also found
in many other states. Realizing that he would need
help, Volansky petitioned Metropolitan Sembratovich
for a priest to aid him. Thus in March of 1887, Rev.
Zenon Liakhovich arrived to assist Volansky. Father
Liakhovich was the first celibate Ukrainian priest in
the United States. He was also the first Ukrainian
priest to be buried on American soil--in St. Michael's
Church cemetery in Shenandoah. With him came Vladimir
Simenovich, a university student from Lviv, the first
known educated Ukrainian layman to settle in the
United States. Until the church building program was
completed in Kingston, Pennsylvania, Volansky assigned
Liakhovich to Shenandoah while he himself set out on a
protracted visitation of immigrant colonies, minister-
ing to their religious needs, organizing congregations
and church committees for the building of future
churches, etc. He travelled through most of the important colonies from New York to Colorado.

On his return he again fixed his residence in
Shenandoah and Father Liakhovich moved to Kingston
when the second Byzantine-Slavic rite church in the
United States, St. Mary's, was completed there. The
untimely death of Liakovich in Wilkes-Barre in November of 1887, however, left Volansky alone again;

4

consequently, in the summer of 1888 he sent Simenovich to Galicia with a petition for a replacement for the late Father Liakhovich. Before the year came to a close Simenovich returned with a new assistant for Volansky, the Rev. Constantine Andrukhovich, who made Kingston his residence. (By this time a third church in America, St. Mary's, was completed in Freeland, Pennsylvania). Within a year, however, primarily as a result of the continued misunderstandings with the Latin rite hierarchy, Metropolitan Sembratovich recalled Volansky to Galicia. During the 1887-1888 coal strike riots in Shenandoah, Volansky was the only local Catholic priest who openly sympathized with and actively supported the striking Slavic mine workers.[22] His radically unorthodox activities during the strike, added to the basic and volatile issue of Volansky being a married cleric, very likely contributed heavily to his recall to Galicia.

By June, 1889 Father Volansky returned to his native land after four and one-half years of pioneering work in the United States, during which time churches were built in Shenandoah, Kingston, Freeland, Olyphant, and Shamokin, all in Pennsylvania, and in Jersey City, New Jersey and Minneapolis, Minnesota.[23] At his Shenandoah parish he organized the first brotherhood, that of St. Nicholas, on January 18, 1885; the first choir; the first reading room; and the first Ukrainian evening school in the United States. In addition, Volansky founded the first Ukrainian newspaper, America, the first issue of which appeared on August 15, 1886. He was also the prime organizer of the fraternal organizations and of the co-operative general stores which were founded for the benefit of the Ruthenian workers and their families.

Obviously, the recall of the very capable and energetic Father Volansky to Galicia was a serious loss to the Ruthenian Catholics in America. An interesting tribute to the first Ukrainian missionary and his dedicated work was supplied by a Shenandoah reporter in an article about Rev. Volansky in 1887.

> Although young, barely more than 30 years of age, tall and slim, though compactly built, and fairly good looking, Father Volansky has no superior as a worker. He scarcely permits himself any rest, so thoroughly is his soul in his work. If life and health stands the test, his religious standing and that of his church will in a

decade or two of years rank high and firm
in America, and he will then be able to
enjoy with ease the honors he will have
richly earned.[24]

Father Volansky did return for a brief period in
1890 in an attempt to clear up the misunderstandings
that had developed in connection with the building
programs in some parishes and with the operation of
the cooperative stores. However, without succeeding
in disentangling the mismanagement of his successor,
Rev. Andrukhovich, Volansky returned to Europe, never
to set foot on American soil again. The misunderstandings unfortunately led to serious internal conflicts which resulted in costly court proceedings
lasting many years.

2. Expansion

From 1889 on priests began to arrive from Europe
in greater numbers. By then, the majority of them
were coming from Transcarpathia rather than from
Galicia. In March of 1889 the fourth priest arrived,
the first apparently from Hungary, Rev. Alexander
Dzubay, who settled in Wilkes-Barre, Pennsylvania. In
the fall he was followed by another Transcarpathian,
Rev. Cyril Gulovich, O.S.B.M., the first Basilian monk
in the United States, who took up residence in Freeland, and later by Gregory Hrushka, a Ukrainian priest
from Galicia, who settled in Jersey City. The entire
territory populated by Ruthenian Catholics was divided
into four districts. Father Andrukhovich, to whom
Volansky had turned over his responsibilities, along
with Father Gulovich and Hrushka, agreed on the following boundaries for the respective parishes:
Shenandoah, with twenty-one surrounding communities,
was to be administered by Andrukhovich; Freeland, with
eighteen surrounding areas, was to be the pastoral
area of Gulovich; Jersey City with nine adjoining set-
tlements, including New York City,[25] was to be minis-
tered to by Father Hrushka; and Olyphant, with eight
neighboring towns was left without a pastor, with the
three priests agreeing to visit this territory in regular rotation. Father Dzubay did not participate in
this arrangement and worked independently in Wilkes-
Barre which was, geographically speaking, within the
Olyphant Parish district.[26]

The above arrangement did not work out well. Before the priests could make a complete round of their

extended parishes a number of new priests arrived
thereby rendering the original parish divisions obso-
lete. Before 1889 came to a close Fathers John
Zapototsky and Victor Tovt arrived from Transcarpathia,
and Rev. Theophan Obushkevich from Galicia. In 1890[27]
Fathers Stephen Jackovich, Alexis Tovt (Toth),
Nicephor Khanat, Eugene Volkay, Gabrial Vislotsky, and
Cornelius and Augustine Lawrysin came from Transcarpathia. They were soon followed by additional
priests from Transcarpathia. Father Andrukhovich was
recalled to Galicia at the beginning of 1892 by Metropolitan Sembratovich, due to the continuous misunderstandings he had with his colleagues and with the
Latin hierarchy. The following year Fathers Ambrose
Poliansky and John Konstankevich arrived from Galicia,
the former making his residence in Pittsburgh and the
latter establishing himself in Shamokin.

Thus in 1894, with over twenty Ruthenian Catholic
priests in the United States only four were from
Galicia.[28] When the first Ukrainian book was published in the United States (an Almanac for 1897
edited by Rev. Dmytriw) it listed a total of twenty-
nine priests in good standing, twenty-four of whom
came from Transcarpathia and five from Galicia.[29]
(see appendix one). They served a population estimated at about 200,000.[30]

It was with the arrival of so many new priests
that a great church building program got under way,
with individual business men very often taking the
initiative.[31] Wherever a number of immigrants were
domiciled in close proximity of one another they soon
gave serious thought to building a church in the hope
that they might be able to obtain a priest that much
more quickly. In the beginning building costs were
nominal. Small wooden chapels and churches were often
built for as little as three to eight thousand dollars.[32] Although there was no uniformity in the
building style, the tendency was to build churches
more or less according to their appearance in the old
country--with cupolas. The early churches were frequently raised a whole story from the ground to allow
for a hall under the church for meetings and for an
evening school. Beginning in 1896, however, some
congregations, like those in Laysering and Mayfield,
Pennsylvania, built separate school buildings.[33]
Whether held in the church halls or in separate buildings, the church evening schools operated, pedagogically speaking, under extremely unfavorable condi-

tions; nevertheless, these schools provided the all-important means by which the children of the immigrants could become acquainted with their heritage.

The funds for the support of the church, school, priest, and the cantor (who at the same time taught in the church school), came from a single tax towards a building fund, monthly dues, and the plate collection during church services. Besides these regular sources, the church committees and organizations held picnics, concerts, banquets, etc., from which the churches might benefit financially. The congregations that did not have their own priests would make an agreement with a neighboring priest to visit them on Sundays or perhaps every other Sunday to celebrate Mass.

Unfortunately, the arrival of so many new priests led not only to a great church building program,[34] but also to a shameful competition among priests and parishes. Thus began a series of scandals, in some instances leading to the organization of a second or even a third parish in the same community. In the small town of Hazleton, Pennsylvania, for example, there were three Ruthenian parishes, each with a priest and a church.[35] On more than one occasion these misunderstandings and conflicts had to be settled by the courts.

3. Factional Disputes

It is imperative, at this point, to provide the reader with an historical background to the internal conflicts among the Ruthenian immigrants and their priests.

In the seventeenth century the old name Ukraine, which dates at least from the twelfth century, took on a special meaning when the eastern territories of modern Ukraine became the center of a new national life under the leadership of the Ukrainian Cossacks (Kozaks).[36] The Ukrainian literary revival of the nineteenth century accepted the name as representing its own national life. Consequently, with the end of the nineteenth century the words Ukraine and Ukrainian were being more and more widely used in Ukrainian and other literatures, thus pushing out other names, including the older traditional name of Rus and Rusyn from the Kievan period.[37] However, in the western areas of Ukraine, in Galicia, and in Transcarpathia, whose political life differed from that in the east, the words Rus and Rusyn (Latinized to Ruthenia and Ruthenian) were retained. In the first place, these lands were not in immediate danger of denationalization by the Russian Empire's policy of Russification, as were the Ukrainian lands in the east; consequently, there was no urgency to break with a name which was also claimed by the Russians. Further, the Austro-Hungarian government fought the use of the new name in their lands in order to prevent the Ruthenians in Galicia and Transcarpathia from associating themselves ethnically with the Ukrainians in the Russian Empire.[38]

Since the early immigrants came from Galicia and Transcarpathia, where the old name Rusyn was commonly in use, there were, broadly speaking, two major groups in the United States. Each of these groups was further sub-divided into various factions. First, there were the immigrants from Galicia, who were divided into the "Ukrainians" and the "Moscophiles". The Ukrainians stood for the interest of the Ukrainian people as distinct from the Russians. They desired to develop the Ukrainian language, literature, and nationality. The Moscophiles imitated all things Russian, and looked toward Moscow as the seat of Slavic culture.[39] Secondly, there were the immigrants from Transcarpathia, among whom three distinct factions existed: (1) the Rusyns who were sympathetic to the Hungarians; (2) those who claimed cultural communion with Russia; and finally, (3) those that claimed cultural communion with the Ukrainians.[40] To a great extent the conflicts among these immigrants were inherited from the political differences which were born in Europe. These were further complicated by the serious religious controversy that the immigrants were experiencing in America. The factional conflicts among the Byzantine-Slavic rite Catholics during their early years in America loosely paralleled the history of the Irish Catholics in the United States between 1815 and 1850, and of the Poles and the Lithuanians between the mid-1860's and 1900. Like the Irish, Poles, and the Lithuanians, the Ruthenians feared that their churches, the center of their social life, were in danger of falling under alien control. The fact that they were Eastern rite Catholics with their own traditional religious laws and customs, which now seemed threatened, made the relationship between themselves and the American Latin rite hierarchy doubly difficult.[41]

The differences between the Galician and the Transcarpathian immigrants, it would seem, were certainly not insurmountable. After all, in the beginning, the Galician immigrants were for the most part Lemky, the immediate neighbors of the Transcarpathians. As a matter of fact, greater cooperation among them appeared to be in prospect when on February 14, 1892, as a result of the efforts of both Transcarpathian and Galician priests, a federation of the fraternal brotherhoods was organized in Wilkes-Barre. That organization, the Sojedinenije Greko-Kaftoliceskich Russkich Bratstv,[42] began publishing its newspaper, the Amerikansky Russky Viestnik on March seventeenth of that year. (The organization and its paper is better known today by its English names: The Greek Catholic Union and the Greek Catholic Union Messenger.) However, in the 1890's neither the Galician nor the Transcarpathian priests displayed the necessary tact, patience, and understanding towards each other's views; consequently, as a result of various misunderstandings the Ukrainians from Galicia under the leadership of Rev. John Konstankevich left the organization in 1893 and a second federation, the Rusky Narodny Soyuz was formed in Shamokin on February 22, 1894.[43] The newspaper Svoboda (Liberty), organized and first published by Rev. Hrushka in Jersey City on September 15, 1893, became the official organ of the Soyuz on May 30, 1894. Thus, from 1894 the conflicts between the Galician and the Transcarpathian immigrants tended to increase, with each fraternal federation through its organ playing a major role. The Sojedinenije and its Viestnik represented the Transcarpathian pro-Hungarian faction, whereas the Soyuz and its organ the Svoboda represented the Galician Ukrainians. (The Soyuz is known today as the Ukrainsky Narodny Soyuz--The Ukrainian National Association.) Other organizations, newspapers, and publications followed, each representing some faction among the immigrants in America.

It was as a result of the bitter conflicts that the Ukrainian immigrants from Galicia began to organize separate parishes. The formation of their own parishes was not difficult, for between 1895 and 1898 seven young celibate priests imbued with the spirit of Ukrainian national revival arrived from Galicia. While seminarians in Lviv they had formed themselves into the so-called "American Circle" with the hope of doing missionary work among the Ukrainian immigrants in America after their ordination. Their arrival signified a radical leadership which, in church matters, sought to work out problems in America through the principle of full democratization of church administration without hindrance from outside forces.[44] These "priest-radicals" were to play an unusually important role in the cultural and national development of the Ukrainian immigrants in the United States.[45]

The first of these priests to arrive was Nestor Dmytriw who settled in Mount Carmel early in 1895, and who soon became the editor of the Svoboda. He was joined in midyear by Rev. Michael Stefanovich who, after a few months in Buffalo, New York, settled in Pittsburgh, Pennsylvania and, before the year ended, by Rev. John Ardan, who made Jersey City his residence. Early in 1897 Rev. Stephen Makar and, toward the end of the year, Fathers Anton Bonchevsky and Michael Pidhorecky joined their former classmates in the New World. Father Makar went to Mount Carmel to replace Dmytriw, who left for Canada in the Spring to minister to the new Ukrainian immigration from Eastern Galicia and Bukovina. Bonchevsky fixed his residence in Ansonia, and Pidhorecky settled in Jersey City, replacing Ardan who moved to Olyphant. In 1898 Rev. Paul Tymkevich arrived, another of the young Ukrainian priests. He soon left for Alberta, Canada, where he remained for almost a year. By the end of 1898, however, both Tymkevich and Dmytriw returned to the United States permanently, with the former taking up residence in Yonkers and the latter in Troy, New York.

The influential role of these young priests in the socio-economic and cultural life of the Ukrainian immigrants is suggested by several of the undertakings of Father Tymkevich in Yonkers. For example, he formed an association which erected a model tenement house, housing thirty-nine families, which was markedly superior to those in the neighborhood. Even more important was another of his undertakings. In 1904 he had gathered under his roof in Yonkers eight orphaned and needy boys from different parts of the country, in order that they could be educated in the superior schools of that city, with the hope that after obtaining a good American education they might provide future leadership for their people.[46]

4. Conflicts with Latin Bishops

The major problems facing the early priest was

11

the lack of any official status for the Byzantine-Slavic rite in the United States and the absence of any normal church organization. Ever since Father Volansky's departure in 1889, there was an increasing number of priests coming to our shores with rights of jurisdiction from their bishops in Europe. However, once in the United States, they frequently worked independently of one another and of the local Ordinary, organizing parishes within the territorial limits of one or of several Latin rite dioceses. Naturally this state of affairs led to internal confusion as well as to serious conflicts with the Latin bishops in whose diocesan territories the priests worked. As previously stated, the majority of the Latin hierarchy and clergy in the United States were unfamiliar with the usages of the Byzantine-Slavic rite. Particularly foreign to Americans was the custom of a married clergy. The early Ruthenian priests, in turn, partially due to their unfamiliarity with the English language, were unable properly to inform the Latin clergy of their Byzantine traditions. The result was often outright hostility on the part of individuals, which led to numerous misunderstandings. The bishops felt that, in order to prevent the undermining of their own authority and the development of chaotic conditions, all priests in the United States must be celibate and subject to them--and they frequently petitioned the Holy See towards that end.

In an attempt to end the near-chaotic conditions, on October 1, 1890, the Holy See issued its first decree relative to the Ruthenian Catholics in America.[47] In accord with the new decree, newly arrived priests were to report to, receive their juristiction from, and remain under the jurisdiction of the Latin rite Ordinary in whose territory they had arranged to reside. Equally important was the requirement that the priests in America were to be celibate, and that the married ones were to be recalled to Europe.[48] The above decree, however, did not produce the desired effect; instead, it added to the difficulties between the two rites. Some of the Ruthenians read into the regulations an attempt to destroy the autonomy of the Byzantine-Slavic rite and to Latinize the Ruthenian Catholics.[49] Consequently, with the growth of radical leadership in the 1890's, many of the congregations chose to retain the ownership of their churches and refused to sign them over to the bishops although, canonically speaking, until 1907 all Byzantine rite churches belonged de jure to the bishops in whose diocese they were located. Thus, a troublesome situation developed where the priests received their jurisdiction from the local bishop on the basis of the documents they carried from Europe, although, the bishop might not have legal ownership of the Church to which he might wish to assign a particular priest. Hence, a priest assigned to a church owned by the congregation found himself in the difficult position of being responsible to two, often conflicting, authorities.

This situation of course, contributed to furthering the already serious internal disagreements among the immigrants--all to the great detriment of the spiritual development of the Ruthenian Catholics in the United States. Consequently, on October 29, 1890, twenty-eight days after the Papal decree, the first gathering of their clergy was held in Wilkes-Barre, where eight of the nine accredited priests in the United States met and decided to petition Rome that, in view of the difficulties between the rites, a Byzantine-Slavic rite Vicar General be appointed with authority over all Catholics of that rite in America.[50] In December of 1891 another important gathering of the clergy was held in Hazleton, Pennsylvania, where a memorandum regarding the position of the Ruthenian Catholics in the United States was formulated and delivered to the Apostolic Delegate by a committee headed by Father Nicephor Khanat. One result of this memorandum was the appointment of Khanat as the acting administrator the following year.[51] His position was mainly that of an intermediary between the Ruthenian priests and the Latin bishops as well as between the discordant factions among the Ruthenians themselves.

The factional conflicts among the priests were now reaching tragic proportions, with cliquish meetings becoming more numerous. Although Father Khanat continued his duties until 1896, his position was more nominal than real. The young "radical" priests from Galicia finally gave up hope of any cooperative action with the priests from the Munkacs Diocese in Hungary.[52]

Early in 1896 specific appeals and recommendations were made by these priests for the formation of their own church administrative organization which would control the priests and their activities, bring order to their church in America, and protect it from the Russophile propaganda of the Russian Orthodox Mission.[53] Finally, on May 30, 1901, clerical and lay delegates met in Shamokin and formed an association of the Ruthenian Church Congregations in the United States and Canada headed by a general committee of three priests and three laymen. The stated goal of the association was "to obtain good priests, to see that in every parish there be order, schools, choirs, reading rooms, and that the poorer chapels obtain the services of a priest at least from time to time, etc."[54] Upon request for a priest from newly organized congregations, the association's clerical committee of six members was to make appointments of priests arriving from Europe, who had to obtain their jurisdiction from the local Latin bishop.

Although only fifteen parishes and ten priests,[55] out of a total of about sixty churches and forty-four priests,[56] accepted the administration of this general committee (the Transcarpathian group soon began its own church organization), it was the first serious attempt to introduce lay control over the church, a principle which troubled the Ruthenian Church in the United States for many years to come.

The height of the movement was reached at the second convention held in Harrisburg, Pennsylvania, on March 26, 1902, where the official name of the association became the Ruthenian Church in America.[57] The characteristic elements of this organization, which lasted until the arrival of the first bishop and the settlement of the religious matters that were canonically the prerogative of the bishop, was its radicalism towards the Latin bishops in particular and towards the hierarchy of the Church in general.[58] The extreme views of some of the young "radical" priests even led to their excommunication and to court fights over churches. The outstanding example is the case of Rev. John Ardan of Olyphant, Pennsylvania and his excommunication by Bishop Michael J. Hoban of Scranton in 1902.[59]

5. New Tensions and Solution

The internal conflicts and the misunderstandings with the hierarchy provided the Russian Orthodox Mission an opportunity for very lively propaganda among the Ruthenians. Taking advantage of the attitude of some of the priests, the Orthodox Mission beginning in 1891, succeeded in establishing itself on a large scale in the eastern states when individual priests and some of their congregations passed over to Orthodoxy. In March of 1891, the Transcarpathian priest Alexis Tovt (Toth) in Minneapolis, became the first priest to turn Orthodox,[60] and in December of 1896 Rev. Gregory Hrushka of Jersey City became the first Ukrainian priest to do the same.[61] Thus, by the turn of the century, the chief problem facing the Ruthenian Catholic priests was combatting the Russian Orthodox propaganda financed by the Tsarist government, which saw in the Ruthenian Church in the United States an important element of the Ukrainian movement.[62] The Russian Mission's proselytizing brought considerable results. By 1901 the Mission had succeeded in converting thirteen Ruthenian Catholic congregations and as many churches to Orthodoxy, with a total population of 6,898 faithful, of whom 2,448 were from Galicia, and 4,450 from Transcarpathia.[63]

The seemingly unending differences with the Latin bishops and the resultant spread of the anti-Roman feeling among the Ukrainian "radical" priests, which reached its climax in 1902, also provided open opportunity for proselytizing by the Episcopalian, Presbyterian, Baptist, and other Protestant groups.[64] Thus, for instance, in the first decade of the current century Presbyterian congregations were established in Pittsburgh, Newark, New Jersey and New York, and a Baptist congregation was organized in Scranton, Pennsylvania.[65]

The many serious problems facing the Ruthenian Catholics, and the numerous letters and memoranda sent to the authorities by the Transcarpathians requesting the appointment of a Vicar General or a Bishop steeped in the Hungarian tradition, prompted the Holy See to seek a definite solution. Early in 1901 there were rumors that the future Apostolic Visitor would be a Transcarpathian from Hungary.[66] The "radical" priests from Galicia made it known that if the appointment of a future Vicar was the result of the Hungarian government's influence, then they would have little faith in such an appointee.[67] Accordingly, when on April 29, 1902, the Right Rev. Andrew Hodobay, Titular Abbot and Canon from the Diocese of Presov in Hungary, arrived in the United States as the Apostolic Visitor to the Ruthenian Catholics, he was to face grave obstacles. The Ukrainian priests strongly opposed Father Hodobay on the ground that his appointment had the full support of the Hungarian government which feared that the immigrants from Hungary would be swayed by the spirit of Ukrainian nationalism diffused by the "radical" priests from Galicia.[68] Thus, Father Hodobay's duties of over-seeing all matters pertaining to the church in America, with the cooperation of the Latin bishops, proved to be difficult to carry out because of the serious split between the Ukrainian and Transcarpathian clergy, the new principle of lay control of the Church, and the continued misunderstandings with the Latin bishops.

The Ruthenian Church had by now reached considerable size and extent in the United States. According to a census made by Father John Korotnoky, who was secretary to Father Hodobay, as of January 11, 1905 there were eighty-nine Ruthenian congregations and sixty-eight priests. Of these congregations, eighty-three had their own church buildings, four had only chapels, and two held services in Latin churches. In addition, seventy-nine of the communities had parish homes, and sixty-nine provided some form of catechetical instructions to a total of about 7,000 children.[69] According to a 1905 almanac of the Sojedinenije, however, there were ninety-five congregations located in ten different states and sixty-seven priests.[70] (See appendix 2). Although an obvious minor discrepancy exists between the two sources in the total number of congregations and priests (due to differences in time of census, arrival and departure of priests, and the fluid condition of some of the congregations), they provide a very close approximation of the size and extent of the Ruthenian Church during Hodobay's mission in the United States.

Shortly after his arrival, Father Hodobay announced that a convocation of priests would be held in Brooklyn, New York on May 21, 1902. The convention which was to decide on local statutes for the Church proved to be ineffective since it was attended only by the thirty-two priests originating from Munkacs and eight from Presov.[71] The Ukrainian priests were not invited to this convocation nor to the succeeding one which was held in Scranton, July 22, and attended only by nineteen of the Transcarpathians.[72] The Ukrainians, therefore, did not participate in the discussions to adopt statutes for the Ruthenian Church in 1902. The friendly relations which existed between the priests from Hungary and Father Hodobay upon his arrival quickly cooled off and became increasingly hostile. A bitter conflict ensued with the Munkacs

16

priests and the Sojedinenije leading the fight against
Father Hodobay.[73] Increasingly, they looked upon
Hodobay as an "exponent of Hungarian political interests"[74] rather than an organizer of the Church.
At his first meeting with the clergy in Brooklyn,
Hodobay had admitted that he came "as the official
representative of the Hungarian Government."[75] In
addition, unfortunately, since the majority of the
Transcarpathian priests were from Munkacs and considered themselves of somewhat aristocratic background, Hodobay's fault was that he was only a "plain
priest from Presov."[76] At the same time his pro-
Magyarism and his slighting of the unfriendly Galician
priests precluded the possibility of obtaining their
support. Hodobay's use of the Magyar language in his
correspondence with the Transcarpathian priests, as
well as his great interest in expanding the number of
Magyar congregations, was considered an indication of
his Magyarization tendency and so earned him the resentment of the priests from Galicia.

The inability of Father Hodobay to gain and keep
the support of all the priests, and to effectively
control their activities, made even more difficult
his relations with the Latin bishops who feared the
chaotic conditions among the Ruthenian Catholics
within their dioceses might lead to a deterioration
of their episcopal authority.[77] Thus Hodobay's mission, to bring order to the Ruthenian Church, was
doomed almost from the start.[78] With increasing protests and complaints against Hodobay to the authorities in Europe, Father Hodobay's mission finally
ended with his recall to Europe in 1907.[79]

From subsequent legislation, however, there is
little doubt, according to Gulovich, that Father
Hodobay's reports to Rome included reference to the
following as the major contributing factors in the
chaotic conditions among the Ruthenian Catholics in
the United States: (1) control of Church and properties by laymen; (2) the scandalous means by which
some priests tried to obtain and hold parishes; and
(3) the almost general disregard for ecclesiastical
authority.[80] On the basis of the insistance of the
Ruthenian bishops in Europe, particularly by the
Most Reverend Count Andrew Sheptytsky, the Metropolitan of Galicia, as well as on the basis of the
reports of Rev. Hodobay, and of the Apostolic Delegate in Washington,[81] Pope Pius X made his decision
to name a bishop for the Ruthenian Catholics in

America. In 1907, the Ruthenian Church in the United
States entered the second phase of its development
with the appointment of Right Rev. Monsignor Soter
Ortynsky, O.S.B.M., as its first bishop.

CHAPTER II

ADMINISTRATION OF THE FIRST BISHOP

1. Pioneering Hardships of a New Bishop

The appointment of a bishop for the Ruthenian Catholics in America altered a traditional principle of the Roman Catholic Church in the West, that all Catholics domiciled in a given territory fell under the jurisdiction of a single Ordinary in that territory. In Eastern Europe, the Near East, and the Middle East, where several different rites of the Church existed in the same territory, dual and triple jurisdictions developed; in Western Europe, however, there was a tradition of almost nineteen hundred years of a single territorial jurisdiction, which naturally made its way to America. It is understandable, therefore, that the American bishops considered it impractical and even unthinkable for the establishment of an Eastern rite diocese in the United States. Herein, incidentally, lies an important cause of the persistent conflicts between the Ruthenian priests, who petitioned for their own separate jurisdiction, and the Latin hierarchy, who could not reconcile themselves with such an intrusion and steadfastly petitioned Rome against such an innovation. In fact, they proposed that all Ruthenians in America transfer to the Latin rite.[1] That the decision to appoint a Ruthenian bishop was finally made by Pope Pius X was primarily the result of the persistent requests, over a period of several years, by Metropolitan Sheptytsky of Galicia.[2] In 1907, Pope Pius X appointed the Metropolitan's candidate, Monsignor Soter Stephen Ortynsky, O.S.B.M., as the first Byzantine-Slavic rite bishop in the United States.

Stephen Ortynsky, who was born in the village of Ortynytsi in Galicia on January 29, 1866, entered the monastic order of St. Basil the Great (O.S.B.M.) in 1884 where he accepted the religious name of Soter. His philosophy and theology studies were completed at Graz University in Austria where he also earned his doctoral degree in Sacred Theology. Ortynsky was ordained a priest by Metropolitan Sembratovich at St. George's Cathedral in Lviv on July 18, 1891.

In succeeding years, his duties included teaching, the priorship of a monastery, and missionary work. His reputation as a Ukrainian patriot, a dedicated missionary, and a talented preacher spread throughout Galicia. On March 8, 1907, he was appointed bishop for the Ruthenians in America and named titular bishop of Daulia by Pius X, being consecrated by Metropolitan Sheptytsky in St. George's Cathedral on May 12, 1907.[3]

The Bishop's first pastoral letter to his priests, dated from Lviv, June 25, 1907 and received in America on August seventh, outlined the new bishop's jurisdiction and his plans for the future.

> As you are aware, my priests, I am a bishop without a diocese. All the Ruthenian Catholics living in the United States have been placed under my jurisdiction and I have been made dependent on the Apostolic Delegate, and through him directly on the Apostolic See. . . . Our earnest efforts shall be directed towards the creation of a full diocese in the shortest possible time which, with God's help, and your wise, honest, and patient collaboration, we will surely attain. I feel that it can not be different at present, because first it will be necessary for me to become an American citizen and only then can we firmly establish the Ruthenian Church and obtain the privileges due her.[4]

Upon his arrival on August 27, 1907, Bishop Ortynsky and his secretary, Rev. Vladimir Petrivsky, were met at Hoboken, New Jersey, by a delegation of priests and laymen led by a committee headed by Revs. Cornelius Lawrisin, Gabriel Chopey, and Joseph Chaplynsky.[5] The Bishop was escorted to New York's St. George's Church at 332-334 East Twentieth Street, where a Moleben service was held and where the following morning Bishop Ortynsky offered his first Pontifical Mass in the United States. On August 29, Ortynsky was escorted to Philadelphia, where the bishop's residence was to be established, and the next day to Washington for an introduction to the Most Rev. Archbishop Diomede Falconio, the Apostolic Delegate. On September 1, the bishop went to South Fork, Pennsylvania, to bless St. Michael's Church on the following day, a duty he had accepted before leaving

Europe.[6] Since the bishop had neither a residence
nor a Cathedral, the priest at South Fork offered his
house to the bishop until suitable quarters could be
arranged. Thus, South Fork became the temporary
residence of Bishop Ortynsky.[7] Early in November the
bishop announced the transfer of his residence to
North Sixty-third street in Philadelphia.[8]

The difficulties that Bishop Ortynsky faced in
his attempt to organize a Ruthenian rite diocese were,
to put it mildly, numerous and serious. In addition
to the generally undisciplined habits of the priests
and congregations (habits acquired from being without
a spiritual head for many years), the new bishop was
also confronted with: Moscophile and Orthodox propaganda of Tsarist Russia, Protestant sectarian influence, increased factional conflicts, and continued
misunderstandings with the Latin hierarchy. All these
problems had to be met and solved before a strong
foundation could be established for the Ruthenian rite
in the United States.[9]

Unfortunately, however, the Apostolic letter _Ea
Semper_,[10] of June 14, 1907, concerning the position
and powers of the new bishop, and the general regulations (constitution) of the Ruthenian rite in the
United States, when published by the Apostolic Delegate on September 16, 1907, had the unintended effect
of intensifying the problems. The papal letter did
not create a Byzantine-Slavic diocese in the United
States; consequently, it did not provide for any
diocesan powers or authority. Although the new bishop
received his primary jurisdiction immediately from
Rome, he was to exercise that jurisdiction as an
auxiliary to the Latin bishops in whose territories
Ruthenian Catholics were domiciled.[11] In addition,
the privilege of the Ruthenian priests to administer
the sacrament of Confirmation at Baptism was to be
withheld.[12] Also married men were not to be ordained
in America, nor were priests to be sent here without
approval.[13] To many Ruthenians _Ea Semper_ appeared to
be an attack on their rite and an obvious victory of
the American hierarchy.[14] At the same time the in-
ferior position of Bishop Ortynsky tended to lead to
even greater factional conflicts.[15]

The news that Ortynsky, a Ukrainian from Galicia,
was appointed Bishop stunned the Magyarized Transcarpathians from Hungary.[16] Most of the priests from
Hungary opposed him because he was Ukrainian, and they

accused him of Latinization and of betraying them because he agreed to be subject to the Latin bishops.[17]
The Galician priests, most of whom recognized Bishop
Ortynsky,[18] were strongly opposed to the regulations
of the letter and prepared petitions for full independent powers for their bishop.[19] Thus, the Ruthenian
dissatisfaction over the Papal letter contributed in
the development of a bitter pro-Ortynsky and anti-
Ortynsky battle.[20] The struggle was spread by the
factional organizations, newspapers, lectures, etc.,
until most of the faithful became involved in these
unfortunate proceedings.[21]

2. Beginnings of His Episcopal Administration

Since Bishop Ortynsky's authority was not accepted by all the priests and since he was under
pressure from the opposition, Ortynsky called a convention of priests, and another of parish delegates,
to introduce himself officially and to hear their
thoughts concerning the organization of a diocese.
The official notices, dated from South Fork September
28, 1907, invited the priests to convene on October
15-16 in St. George's Church in New York City and the
parish delegates were to meet there on the succeeding
two days.[22] It was hoped that these steps would help
nullify the major internal problems. The agenda for
the priests Convention illustrates the specific internal administrative problems faced by the new bishop.

1. Stabilization of boundaries for the
   existing parishes.
2. Organization of new parishes.
3. The security of priests in old age or
   in event of illness.
4. Division of all churches into Deaneries.
5. Division of all parishes into classes.
6. Missionary priests and chapels.
7. Parish schools and Ruthenian-American
   textbooks and catechisms.
8. Schools for cantors.
9. Normalization of salaries and religious
   ceremonies.
10. Home for orphans and the poor.
11. Sisters, and Wards for children.
12. Residence (bishop's), cathedral, and a
    Ruthenian-American seminary.
13. Election of a committee for the pre-
    paration of: a) a History of the

Ruthenian Church in America. b) Schemat-
ism (List of churches, membership, organizations, etc.) for 1908.
14. The material security of the Ruthenian
Bishop.[23]

Although some felt there was insufficient time to
prepare for the gathering,[24] the convention, attended
by seventy-six priests,[25] benefitted the bishop in
that it voted specific and favorable action on each of
the topics on the agenda. For example, the bishop's
material position was improved when the convention
voted a five per-cent cathedraticum (brutto) for the
support of the bishop. The administration of the
Church was further centralized when the convention
voted to divide the territory of the United States
into nine Deaneries, namely: Shenandoah, New York,
Ansonia, Philadelphia, Wilkes-Barre, Pittsburgh,
Boston, Chicago, and Cleveland.[26]

The bishop's announcement of the meeting of
parish delegates included the following subject matter
for the conference.

1. Churches, registered and non-registered.
2. Religious education of children, their
   higher education, and a school scholarship fund.
3. The support of the Bishop.
4. Cathedral, residence (bishop's), and
   the Ruthenian-American seminary.
5. Parish schools.
6. Orphanage for the poor and crippled.
7. Sisters, and Wards for children.
8. Schools for cantors.
9. The building of new churches with the
   approval of the Bishop only.
10. Unauthorized collections in the local
    parish for all sorts and purposes.
11. Slander in the newspapers.
12. Ruthenian organizations.
13. The rights of citizenship.[27]

As in the case of the priests convention the
gathering of the parish delegates[28] also proved to be
beneficial. For example, the delegates also voted for
the five per-cent cathedraticum, and they recommended
that all Ruthenian Churches be signed over to the jurisdiction of Bishop Ortynsky.[29] It is interesting to
note that the delegates of this convention went on

record with the recommendation that those who did not intend to return to Europe should attempt to become American citizens.

The practical application of these and other principles accepted by both conventions was another matter, however, and the problems of jurisdiction continued to a lesser or greater degree throughout Bishop Ortynsky's episcopate.[30] Administratively speaking, there were three types of Ruthenian churches in the United States at the time of Ortynsky's arrival: churches and priests under Latin bishops, independent churches and priests, and independent churches with priests under Latin bishops. At the beginning of 1908, there were about 120 Ruthenian churches, twenty-four of these (mostly Transcarpathian) were under the jurisdiction of Latin bishops,[31] while the remainder, and about an equal number of priests, remained independent of the Latin bishops, but were, generally, willing to accept Ortynsky's jurisdiction. The jurisdictional problem actually became more complicated as some of the Ruthenian churches refused to recognize the authority of Bishop Ortynsky. Consequently a situation developed whereby within the territory of a particular diocese Bishop Ortynsky had control of some of the Ruthenian churches whereas the local Ordinary had jurisdiction over others. This situation resulted in a divided jurisdiction which often led to chaotic conditions.[32] Under the circumstances it seemed certain that the legal transfer of all church property to the jurisdiction of Bishop Ortynsky, which in itself was a complicated procedure, would relieve the misunderstandings arising out of the divided jurisdiction.[33] Despite the many serious obstacles confronting him, Bishop Ortynsky commenced to bring order into the Ruthenian Church in the United States by laying the groundwork for strong diocesan organization.

At first Ortynsky became the rector of the Holy Ghost Church at 1925 W. Passyunk Ave., in Philadelphia.[34] Next he chose the little church of St. Michael the Archangel at Ninth and Buttonwood Sts.,[35] which incidentally was much nearer to his residence at 1105 North 63rd Street. Finally, late in 1908, Bishop Ortynsky bought the former St. Jude's Episcopal Church in the 800 block of North Franklin Street which, after refitting, was consecrated as the Cathedral of the Immaculate Conception.[36] The adjoining building, at 816 North Franklin Street, became the bishop's permanent residence. Thus, Franklin Street was soon to

become the center of the religious life of the
Ruthenian Catholics in the United States, as the town
of Shenandoah was its original center in the 1880's.
The new cathedral was solemnly consecrated in elabo-
rate services on October 2, 1910 by Metropolitan
Sheptytsky and Bishop Ortynsky, assisted by 16
Ruthenian priests, and participated in by distinguished members of the Latin hierarchy and priesthood,
about 50 other Ruthenian priests, other dignitaries,
and great numbers of the faithful. In its comprehensive account of the consecration ceremonies, The
Catholic News reported that,

> It was a sight never before seen in America
> in which a Greek Archbishop and Bishop, as
> consecrating prelates, as well as the Apos-
> tolic Delegate, Archbishop Diomede Falconio,
> Cardinal Vannutelli, Archbishop Ryan, Bishop
> Prendergast, and others took part. It was a
> mingling of the Greek Catholic and Roman
> Catholic hierarchy and priesthood in one
> solemn ceremony, such as has never before
> been witnessed in the United States.[37]

The above report of the ceremonies also includes
the following description of the interior of the new
cathedral, especially of the altar and its tabernacle,
which the writer feels would interest the modern
reader.

> It is the only episcopal home of the
> Ruthenian Greek Catholics in America, and
> has been lavishly decorated with mural
> paintings by a fine Ruthenian artist. The
> Altar itself is of the Greek style, per-
> fectly square and so arranged that the
> clergy can easily pass all around it in
> procession. The tabernacle, situated some-
> what in the centre, is in the form of a
> miniature Greek church in the Byzantine
> style, whose domes and cupola were sur-
> mounted with tiny electric lights.[38]

The Eucharistic Congress which was held in
Montreal, Canada, on September 6-12, 1910, provided
Metropolitan Sheptytsky with the opportunity to visit
the United States and to acquaint himself with the
problems facing his friend Bishop Ortynsky. As previously indicated, Ortynsky was experiencing great
difficulties at this time, particularly the strong

opposition from many of the Magyarized Transcarpathian clergy. According to Brother Joseph Grodsky, O.S.B.M., who accompanied the Metropolitan in his visit, Ortynsky himself, among others, requested that the Metropolitan come to America, since he alone was considered able to solve the problems that seemed to defy solution.[39] Thus, on August 23, several weeks before the Eucharistic Congress was to meet, the Metropolitan arrived and was met at the Hoboken pier by a large delegation of the Ukrainian and Transcarpathian faithful and clergy, and by Bishop Ortynsky.[40] After a hotel reception and dinner in New York, the Metropolitan was escorted to St. George's Church where Moleben services were held by the Metropolitan, assisted by Bishop Ortynsky and other priests.

The Metropolitan's arrival was a joyous event, however, the hope that the great dignity of Sheptytsky would bring about an end to the opposition to Ortynsky was not fulfilled. In an audience with the Metropolitan in Philadelphia on November 30th, thirty-six of the forty-six Transcarpathian priests who had signed a petition voiced their strong dissatisfaction with Bishop Ortynsky, and requested that the Metropolitan aid them in obtaining their own bishop.[41] In an interview the following day Sheptytsky appeared disturbed about the matter, he denied the validity of the charges that the priests made against Ortynsky at the conference, stating that Bishop Ortynsky's actions "have been discussed and found not objectionable."[42] Obviously the meeting with the Metropolitan did not materially improve the relations between most of the Transcarpathian priests and their Bishop.[43] Moreover, the Sojedenenije and its publication **Viestnik** continued their attacks.

The Metropolitan made several official visitations to Ruthenian parishes in the East, such as the Pittsburgh area, Buffalo and Syracuse, before leaving with Ortynsky for the Eucharistic Congress in Montreal, where they represented the Ruthenian Church. Upon the completion of the Congress, Sheptytsky and Ortynsky visited a number of parishes farther west like those in Chicago, Whiting (Indiana) and Cleveland, before returning to Philadelphia.[44] After blessing the site of the proposed seminary in Yorktown, Virginia, on September 28, consecrating the new cathedral on October 2, and making other visitations, the Metropolitan left for Canada on October 5, where he remained until the latter part of November.

In Canada, the Metropolitan continued his serious discussions with the Canadian bishops concerning the possibility of the appointment of a bishop for the Ukrainian Canadians.[45]

3. Organizational Accomplishments

The first major institution that Bishop Ortynsky established in the United States was an orphanage for the care of children. In 1911, partially with his own personal funds, the bishop bought a building at 7th and Parrish Streets for that purpose and requested Sheptytsky's aid in obtaining the Sisters of St. Basil the Great (O.S.B.M.) to direct it. Mother Helen (Lanhevych) from the Convent in Yavoriv, Galicia, was the first to volunteer for this missionary work. Mother Helen, together with Sisters Euphemia and Paphnutia and two candidates, arrived in New York on December 2, 1911.[46] The need for more sisters soon became obvious and Mother Helen's request for additional sisters brought about the arrival, in November of 1912, of Sisters Apolinaria and Mytrodora from the Convent in Yavoriv and Sister Makryna from the Convent in Slovitsky, both in Galicia. Mother Helen also accepted several candidates, thus with this extra force the work progressed so rapidly that in the fourth year of operation there were 121 children in St. Basil's Orphanage.[47] To help support the sisters and the orphanage Bishop Ortynsky founded a church supply store, a printing press, book store, and eventually a rug and carpet shop. It was hoped that these associated institutions would eventually become a source of permanent income and thus relieve the sisters from begging for their support and the support of the orphans, as well as to reduce the bishop's financial burden.[48] In 1912 the bishop bought a farm in Chesapeake, Maryland, where the small orphans spent their summer vacations.

The orphanage became an important source of future vocations to the priesthood. The older boys were soon removed from the tutelage of the sisters and moved to the bishop's house and placed under the supervision of Rev. O. Kulmatytsky and Messrs. V. Semotiuk and J. Lysak.[49] Facetiously, Bishop Ortynsky liked to call this boys' orphanage his "minor seminary". From the very beginning Ortynsky had realized the need for the establishment of a seminary for the training of an American born Ruthenian priesthood, as recommended, it might be noted, in the Apostolic

27

letter _Ea Semper_[50] in 1907. In 1910 plans were formulated to build a seminary in Yorktown, Virginia.[51] Apparently, however, Ortynsky changed his plans, and considered establishing a seminary in Washington, D.C., affiliated with Catholic University. Bishop Ortynsky even thought of gaining financial support of the Hungarian government for the project. Count Tisza, the Hungarian Prime Minister, however, was strongly against the project, fearing that the Ruthenians from Hungary's Transcarpathia might thereby become estranged from their mother country. The Count wanted certain assurances from Ortynsky,[52] commitments which the bishop was not willing to make.[53] These relations were interrupted by the First World War. Finally, the sudden death of Bishop Ortynsky in 1916 brought to an end the hope of establishing a seminary in the immediate future.

While plans for a seminary were in progress, Ortynsky chose to send his seminarians to St. Mary's Seminary of the Sulpician Fathers in Baltimore to provide training for his future priests. The candidates attended the seminary's St. Charles College after which they continued Theology at St. Mary's, the seminary proper. The director of the seminarians at St. Mary's was the pastor of St. Michael the Archangel's Church in Baltimore. It was Bishop Ortynsky's wish that the pastor of the Baltimore parish should be a priest who could direct the seminarians in the spirit of the Byzantine-Slavic rite.[54] The pastor would have to teach the students the history of the Ruthenian Church, the Church Slavonic language, rites, and church music. To this important task, Ortynsky appointed Rev. Constantine Kuryllo.

Shortly after his arrival in the United States, Bishop Ortynsky saw the great need for cultural and educational organizations and publications to further the enlightenment of the immigrants. In the beginning, Ortynsky took an active role in the work of the existing organizations, particularly in the friendly Soyuz. In 1908 the bishop was made the patron of the Soyuz. This show of good will, however, inadvertently led to a misunderstanding between the Soyuz and Ortynsky. It seemed inappropriate for a Catholic bishop to be the patron of an organization to which non-Catholics belonged. Thus the idea was born to change the Soyuz into an organization for Catholics only.[55] On the advice of the bishop's Consultors, according to Rev. Peter Poniatishin (one of the consultors) an attempt was made to change the Soyuz into an organization for Catholics during the Eleventh Convention held in Cleveland on September 20-23, 1910.[56] These events created much trouble among the Ukrainian Americans and, incidentally, led to harsh polemics between the supporters of the bishop and of the Soyuz. Although the change was approved by the majority of the delegates, it was not put into effect due to legal technicalities, according to the organizations' officers.[57] Bishop Ortynsky was naturally displeased with the result; he left the Soyuz, and decided to form separate religious organizations. Consequently, several new religious associations and publications were begun or were supported by him.

In 1912, Ortynsky founded one of his most successful organizations, a new exclusively Catholic beneficial association, the Provydinia (Providence). He was greatly aided in the organization by Rev. Nicholas Pidhorecky, of New York, and Rev. Alexander Ulitsky, from Jersey City, who did the spade work in bringing the association to life by organizing local branches, first in New York, then in Newark, Jersey City, and Yonkers, and by Rev. Eronim Barysh from Pittsburgh, who wrote the first statutes which united the several branches into a single organization called the Providence Association. Important contributions to the formation of the Providence were also made by Revs. Peter Poniatishin, Roman Zalitach, Alexander Pavliak, Vladimir Dovhovich and others. Rev. Barysh became the new organization's first President; he became ill, however, and was soon succeeded by Rev. Pidhorecky. The headquarters of the new organization remained in New York until 1914, when they were moved to Philadelphia, the residence of the Bishop. Several reasons prompted the move: it was felt that the organization's growth potential would be limited if it remained in New York, since all of the local branches in the vicinity were already brought into the organization; the State of Pennsylvania offered more favorable charter provisions; moving its headquarters to the city of the bishop's domicile would give the organization added prestige; lastly, it was believed that without its own publication the growth of the association would thereby also be limited.[58] The founding of its own paper was financially impossible. In Philadelphia, however, the Sisters of St. Basil the Great had published the Ukrainian weekly America (Amerika) since 1914; this could become the publicity agent of the association.[59] From the time the Provi-

dence moved to Philadelphia it began to pay part of
the expenses for the publication of <u>America</u>, and in
return the paper became its official organ.[60]

Thus, the Providence Association was chartered by
the State of Pennsylvania in 1914 with Bishop Ortynsky,
M. K. Kullo, Joseph P. Loftus, and Revs. Basil
Stetsiuk and Vladimir Derzyruka as the chartered
organizers.[61] Until 1916 the Providence Association
remained predominantly localized, but the move to
Philadelphia provided the impetus for expansion into
a strong national organization, although it was still
financially dependent on the Bishop.

4. Creation of a New Exarchy

Despite the important accomplishments of Ortynsky
there remained a major obstacle in his attempts to
establish discipline and order among the Ruthenian
Catholics. That obstacle was the lack of an independent diocese which meant that Bishop Ortynsky was
hindered in his work because his powers of jurisdiction were incomplete. This situation was rectified by
the decisions of the Holy See on May 28, 1913, when
the Holy Father conferred upon Bishop Ortynsky full
and ordinary jurisdiction over all the faithful and
clergy of the Ruthenian rite in the United States.[62]
The American Ruthenians were thereby granted complete
independence from the American Latin hierarchy.[63]
Rev. Joseph F. X. Healy wrote in 1935 that the
founding of the new exarchy

> . . . was intended by the sovereign Pontiff
> as a mark of especial grace toward a people
> which, holding fast to the Roman allegiance
> despite terrific opposition, had built up a
> splendid ecclesiastical organization in a
> foreign land. It was designed also as the
> most expeditious means of forestalling
> complexities likely to arise through in-
> sufficient familiarity with the laws and
> customs of the Eastern Church.[64]

According to official statistics, the newly created Byzantine-Slavic rite Exarchy (missionary diocese), with its seat in Philadelphia,[65] contained 152
churches with resident priests, 43 missions, and a
total of 154 priests serving an estimated 500,000
Ruthenian Catholics.[66] Although their churches or
missions were to be found in eighteen different

states, 103 of them were concentrated in Pennsylvania. Nineteen congregations were listed in the State of New York, thirteen in Ohio,[67] and eleven in New Jersey. None of the remaining fourteen states in which Ruthenian churches are listed (Connecticut, Delaware, Illinois, Maryland, Massachusetts, Michigan, Minnesota, Missouri, New Hampshire, North Dakota, Rhode Island, West Virginia, and Wisconsin), had more than five congregations within their borders.[68] The new exarchy was divided into the following eleven deaneries, the location of which provide additional indication of the importance of Pennsylvania in the early history of the Byzantine-Slavic Church in the United States.

Deanery	Dean
Boston	Rev. Stephen Vashchyshyn
Chicago	Rev. Valentine Balogh
Cleveland	Rev. Demetrius Dobrotvor
Homestead, Pennsylvania	Very Rev. Alexander Holoshnay
New York	Very Rev. Nicholas Pidhorecky
Philadelphia	Very Rev. Augustine Komporday
Pittsburgh	Very Rev. Vladimir Dovhovich
Scranton	Very Rev. Michael Jackovich
Shenandoah	Rev. Leo Levitsky
South Fork, Pennsylvania	Rev. Elias Goidics
Syracuse	Rev. Alexander Prystay[69]

Bishop Ortynsky appointed Very Rev. Alex Dzubay as his Vicar General, and named the Very Revs. Valentine Gorzo, Nicholas Pidhorecky, Victor Mirossay, Peter Poniatishin, Nicholas Chopey, and Vladimir Dovhovich as the Diocesan Consultors.[70] Other leading officials named to the various curias of the new diocese were Very Revs. John Konstankevich, Joseph Hanulya, Alexander Ulitsky, Alexander Holoshnay, Michael Jackovich, Joseph Chaplinsky, Augustine Komporday, Nicholas Strutynsky, and Philemon Tarnavsky.[71] The formal installation of the various officials of the new diocese were held at the Cathedral of the Immaculate Conception on March 26, 1914.[72]

After receiving his full ordinary powers Bishop Ortynsky prepared to make his episcopal visit to Rome. Before his departure Ortynsky named his Vicar General as the administrator of the diocese in his absence, and the Very Rev. Consultor, Augustine Komparday, as the Chancelor.[73] On June 2, 1914, the Bishop left for

Europe, with Rev. Vladimir Derzyruka accompanying him as his secretary.[74]

During Bishop Ortynsky's sojourn in Europe the First World War suddenly erupted; consequently, he was forced to cut short his visit. He returned to the United States in August, the same month that the details of the new relationship between the Latin Catholics and the Byzantine-Slavic rite Catholics were clarified. These relations were spelled out by the Apostolic constitution Cum Episcopo,[75] dated August 17, 1914; the decree was to remain in effect for ten years. Although it has since been superseded, many of its basic regulations remain effective to the present day. The new regulations contained in Cum Episcopo were intended, by clarifying the issues involved, to bring to an end the practical difficulties which often led to jurisdictional differences between the Latin and Byzantine rites. For example: The Ruthenians were prohibited from changing their rite without the permission of the Sacred Congregation of the Propagation of Faith for Oriental Rites;[76] the children of families of mixed rites automatically belonged to the rite of the father;[77] and baptism by another rite did not change the status of the baptized person.[78] Obviously, these and other specific regulations were at least partially intended to safeguard the Eastern rite minority from being overwhelmed by the predominantly Latin character of American Catholicism. Understandably, the new regulations did not automatically bring to an end all the jurisdictional difficulties between the Latin and the Ruthenian Catholics in the United States. They did, however, lay down the legal basis for a less inequitable working out of the complex relations between the rites. Thus, the first Papal constitution for the Ruthenians in the United States, Ea Semper, issued by Pope Pius X in 1907 on the occasion of the appointment of the first Byzantine rite bishop, and which had evoked general disappointment from the Ruthenians, was now superseded by the new constitution, Cum Episcopo, on the occasion of the creation of an independent Byzantine-Slavic rite missionary diocese in 1913.

Like its predecessor, the new constitution did not meet with universal approval. The establishment of an independent exarchy meant an obvious improvement in the relations with the Latin hierarchy, but some writers continued to voice strong dissatisfaction with the autonomy accorded to the Ruthenians.[79] Their arguments, mostly relative to the superiority of the Latin rite, usually created resentment and fear on the part of the Ruthenians of the dominant Latin Catholicism, even though most of those arguments can be dissolved by a single sentence from a well-known writer on the Eastern Churches. "The prevailing Latin uniformity of today is simply the result of historical events: it might just as well have been Greek; in another two thousand years it may be Chinese."[80] Nevertheless, the strong views of some writers helped to continue and even to spread misunderstanding between the Latin and Eastern rite Catholics in the United States long after the publication of Cum Episcopo.

The misunderstanding between the Latin and the Eastern Catholics was an important factor in the schism of many Ruthenians into Orthodoxy since the 1890's. With the arrival of Bishop Ortynsky in 1907, however, the spread of internal conflicts as well as the intensification of Orthodox proselytizing, increased the number of Ruthenian Catholics seceding to the Russian Orthodox Church. The struggle with the Russian Orthodox, particularly over the attempts to appropriate Ruthenian Catholic Churches, took the most serious proportions, even involving the use of excommunication[81] and court suits.[82] The secession movement reached its apogee in 1916 when the Russian Holy Synod decided to consecrate the Very Rev. Alexander Dzubay as the first dissident bishop. Rev. Dzubay had seceded shortly after Bishop Ortynsky's death and on August 19, 1916 was consecrated Bishop of Pittsburgh by the Russian Orthodox Metropolitan, Prince Evdokim Meschersky, in St. Nicholas Russian Cathedral in New York City.[83]

The importance of the Ruthenians in the growth of the Russian Orthodox Church in America is not to be overlooked. According to Russian Orthodox sources, in 1914, shortly after Bishop Ortynsky received his full ordinary powers over the Ruthenian Catholics in the United States, 43,000 Ruthenians from Galicia, Transcarpathia and Bukovina were registered members of the Russian Orthodox Church in America; which had a total membership of only 100,000.[84] Virtually all of the 43,000 from Austria-Hungary were former Ruthenian Catholics who passed into Orthodoxy because of the quarrels with the Latin hierarchy or with Bishop Ortynsky (or other internal conflicts) and the increased propagandizing activities of the Russian

Orthodox Church. Archbishop Evdokim, for example,
taking advantage of the serious differences between
Bishop Ortynsky and many of the Transcarpathian
priests sent a letter to the Viestnik, which was
leading the fight against Ortynsky, in which he attempted to sway the Transcarpathian people into Russian Orthodoxy.[85]

5. War Developments and the Bishop's Death

With the outbreak of the First World War, for the
first time the Ruthenians in the United States found
themselves in a position of leadership in the affairs
of their kinsmen in Europe. Bishop Ortynsky, for
instance, was of the opinion that the immigrants must
take the lead in the affairs of their people, at least
until that time when those in their native lands could
act in their own behalf.[86] Consequently, he activated
a general collection of funds to aid the victims of
the war, and he was primarily responsible for the
organization of the Ruthenian National Rada (council)
at a gathering of delegates from Galician and Transcarpathian parishes held in Philadelphia on December
8, 1914. The Council was to coordinate the efforts of
all the Ruthenian Catholic organizations in behalf of
their people in Europe who were suffering because of
the war.[87]

Thus, as a result of the events taking place in
the European lands of their origin during the First
World War, the first impetus was provided for the
founding of national political organizations among the
American Ruthenians. Particularly was this in evi-
dence with those originating from Galicia which ever
since the middle of the 19th century had been a source
of Ukrainian national revival. It was in 1914, for
instance, that the leading organization of the immigrants from Galicia, the Ruthenian National Association (Soyuz), officially changed its name to the
present Ukrainian National Association. Even the less
politically conscious American Galicians now embraced
the national name "Ukrainian" in place of the old name
"Ruthenian", by which they were known.[88]

The hard work, the endless difficulties, and
fights against him strained Ortynsky's nerves and
undermined his health. On March 16, 1916, Bishop
Ortynsky became ill with pneumonia, and died eight
days later. The immediate area surrounding the
bishop's cathedral and residence on North Franklin

Street in Philadelphia, the quadrangle formed by
Brown, Seventh, Parish and Eights Streets, was deeply
saddened. Here were located the Sisters of St.
Basil's Convent, the Orphanage, the Orphanage press,
the Providence Association, the newspaper _America_,
and the homes housing many of the people having direct
relations with these and other institutions founded or
supported by the Bishop.

On March 30th the final funeral services were
held at the Immaculate Conception Cathedral in the
presence of the Apostolic Delegate, Archbishop Edmond
F. Prendergast of Philadelphia, three Bishops, Monsignori, numerous clergy, and other honored guests, with
an estimated 10,000 to 15,000 people jamming Franklin
Street outside the cathedral for a glimpse of the
funeral ceremonies.[89] There were numerous Ruthenian
organizations represented. Bishop Nykyta Budka, the
Ukrainian bishop from Canada, whom many thought would
succeed Ortynsky, was to have been the celebrant of
the Requiem Mass. In his absence, however, Very Rev.
Alexander Dzubay, the Vicar General, was the celebrant
with Revs. Levitsky and Chorniak serving as the dea-
cons. Eulogies were delivered by Rev. Joseph
Chaplinsky, former superior of Ortynsky; Rev.
Valentine Gorzo, a Transcarpathian priest; Monsignor
Michael J. Lavelle representative of the Archbishop
of New York, who had, incidentally, welcomed Bishop
Ortynsky on his arrival in the United States in 1907;
and Rev. Nicholas Pidhorecky, who thanked the gathering for their participation in the funeral rites.[90]
Following the Divine Liturgy and the final procession,
the bishop's remains were laid to rest under the side
altar of St. Josephat in the Cathedral of the Immaculate Conception.

The more important accomplishments of the first
bishop have been reviewed. It should be added that,
in spite of the almost constant internal opposition
and the strong Orthodox and Russophile propaganda
against him Ortynsky succeeded in bringing about
greater discipline within the Church, and a great
increase in the number of churches and priests under
his jurisdiction, from about 120 churches and priests
in 1908[91] to 152 churches with resident priests (in
addition to many missions) and 161 priests in 1916.[92]
In short, a strong foundation had been erected upon
which Ortynsky's successor could continue to build.

Upon Bishop Ortynsky's death, the Apostolic

Delegate, Archbishop Bonzano, telegraphed for instructions concerning the steps to be taken relative to the naming of an administrator of the exarchy. The action taken changed the administrative character of the Ruthenian Church in the United States and laid the foundations for the creation of separate exarchies for the people originating from Galicia and those whose origin was Transcarpathia.

CHAPTER III

THE INTERREGNUM

1. The struggle with Russian Orthodoxy

Following the death of Bishop Ortynsky the Apostolic Delegate, the Most Reverend Giovanni Bonzano, proposed that the consultors of the exarchy choose two candidates for administrators, one candidate for the Ukrainians from Galicia and the second for the Transcarpathian Rusyns and others from Hungary. The Ukrainian members of the consistory at the time were: Very Revs. Peter Poniatishin, Nicholas Pidhorecky, Vladimir Dovhovich, and Alexander Ulitsky. The Transcarpathian members were: Very Revs. Alexander Dzubay, Vicar General of the exarchy; Valentine Balogh, Chancellor of the exarchy; Valentine Gorzo, Nicholas Chopey, and Victor Mirossay.[1] The Transcarpathian consultors chose Rev. Gabriel Martyak, pastor from Lansford, Pennsylvania, as their candidate, whereas the Ukrainian consultors elected Rev. Peter Poniatishin, pastor in Newark, New Jersey.

On April 11, 1916, Revs. Martyak, Poniatishin and Valentine Balogh, the Chancellor, met with the Apostolic Delegate in Washington, D. C. who advised them that the Holy See had appointed two administrators for the Ruthenian Church in the United States, although the exarchy was to remain one. It was obvious that the creation of two separate administrations was a move on the part of the Vatican to help satisfy the wishes of the Transcarpathian priests who for many years had been dissatisfied with a bishop of Ukrainian stock and had often requested their own bishop. Each administrator received episcopal jurisdiction, with the exception that neither had the power to ordain candidates to the priesthood nor the faculty to bless Holy Oils. Rev. Poniatishin's jurisdiction was over the faithful who originated in Galicia, whereas Rev. Martyak's powers extended over those who originated in Hungary.[2] In mixed parishes of Ukrainians and Transcarpathians the two administrators were to agree between themselves regarding the appointment of pastors and other matters of parish administration. In the event that the administrators could not agree, then the Apostolic Delegate was to make the decision. The Apostolic Delegate instructed the administrators to remain in their respective parishes, for it was not known how long the administrations would continue. From the conversation with the Delegate it could be construed that it would not be long before the appointment of a new bishop.[3] The two new administrators instructed the clergy to continue to refer all administrative matters to the chancery at 818 North Franklin Street, where Rev. Michael Guryansky, appointed secretary of the exarchy by Bishop Ortynsky before his death, would continue his duties.[4] The ostensibly temporary administrations lasted eight years and five months finally ending with the arrival of new bishops in August of 1924.

With the appointment of two administrators and the creation of two separate ecclesiastic administrations for the Byzantine-Slavic Church in 1916, the attention of our history will turn specifically to the further developments within that half of the exarchy under the administration of Very Rev. Poniatishin, whose jurisdiction applied to the Ukrainian Catholics originating from Galicia and Bukovina. It was from the Ukrainian half of the exarchy that the Holy See, in 1958, created the Byzantine rite Ukrainian Ecclesiastical Province of Philadelphia. That half of the exarchy which was administered by Very Rev. Martyak, whose jurisdiction included the Transcarpathians and others originating from Hungary, developed later into the present Byzantine Ruthenian Ecclesiastical Province of Pittsburgh (formerly Munhall, Pa.), and its history is outside the scope of this study.

The administrator for the American Ukrainian Catholics, Very Rev. Peter Poniatishin was born in Galicia on July 15, 1877. After finishing his secondary education in Ternopil, he entered the seminary in Lviv where he completed his studies in philosophy. He continued his studies in theology in Innsbruck, Freiburg, and later in Paris. He was ordained to the priesthood by Metropolitan Sheptytsky in Lviv on July 11, 1902. Father Poniatishin arrived in the United States in 1903 and served as pastor in Ramey, Pennsylvania, until 1907. For three years he was pastor in Elizabeth, New Jersey, until he was transferred to Newark, New Jersey in 1910. In addition, Rev. Poniatishin was very active in the affairs of the American Ukrainians, contributing articles and serving in editorial and directorial capacities for Ukrainian publications. As previously noted, he became a diocesan consultor under Bishop Ortynsky.[5]

The major problems facing the new administration of Father Poniatishin were, in many ways, those with which Bishop Ortynsky was greatly concerned. The official report of the convention of the Ukrainian priests which was held on October 10, 1916, in New York lists the problems of schism, the seminary, schools, orphanage, and people's politics, as the major topics discussed.[6] The convention unanimously accepted the following resolutions:

1. To organize a Missionary Association under the patronage of Sts. Peter and Paul to defend our Church against our enemies.
2. To create a School Commission.
3. To publicize the need of a Seminary.
4. To make a collection each month in all parishes for the Orphanage. In addition each priest to contribute $3.00 each month.
5. Whereas, the present political situation demands the unified efforts of all the people in a dignified and conscientious work, and since the Federation of Ukrainians in the United States is leading a narrow partisan policy, harmful to the Church and the people, the general convention of Ukrainian priests has decided to organize the Ukrainian Rada in America.[7]

In addition, the convention also approved several other proposals; for instance, a plea to petition the Holy See through the Apostolic Delegate for an early nomination of a bishop, and a plan for each priest to contribute $1.00 a month to the administration for the support of ailing priests.[8]

According to Rev. Poniatishin himself, the most serious concern of the Ukrainian Church at this time, as it had been since the 1890's, was the very active Russian Orthodox Mission,[9] which, through the material aid of the Russian Holy Synod in St. Petersburg, now stood on firm ground in the United States. According to the census of religious bodies in the United States, prior to the fall of the Tsarist regime in 1917, the Holy Synod of Russia spent $77,850 annually from the Tsar's treasury for the support of the

Russian Orthodox Mission in America.[10] The Mission's
activities were aimed primarily in the direction of
the Ukrainian and Transcarpathian Catholics from
Austria-Hungary.

After the death of Bishop Ortynsky, the activities of the Russian Mission among the Ukrainian Catholics were expanded. Consequently, the conduct of the
Russian missionaries helped to decide the program of
Poniatishin's administration which, according to Rev.
Poniatishin himself, was "to defend our church by all
means before Russian inroads among our people."[11]

As an illustration of the character and the
seriousness of the struggle with the Russian missionaries, Poniatishin points to the case in Butler, Pennsylvania, where the Russian Mission attempted to take
control of a Ukrainian Catholic church by appointing
an Orthodox priest as pastor when a vacancy occurred.
To remove the Orthodox priest from their church the
Ukrainian Catholics appealed to the courts where the
litigations continued for over two years, finally
ending in a victory for the Ukrainians.[12] That court
decision helped to deter further overt attempts to
usurp Ukrainian Catholic churches. In addition, after
the Russian Revolution broke out in March of 1917,
Russian Orthodoxy in the United States became greatly
weakened internally for lack of financial aid from
Petrograd; consequently, it stopped being as serious a
problem to the Ukrainian Church as it had been.[13] At
the same time, Rev. Poniatishin's success in obtaining
an amendment to the religious corporation law in the
State of New York relative to the incorporation of
Ukrainian Catholic churches, which became law on May 3,
1917,[14] was a major step in protecting church property
from usurpation in that state. It is noteworthy that
the Latin bishops were very sympathetic and helpful to
Father Poniatishin in the passage of the law, particularly Bishop Thomas F. Kusack of Albany and Bishop
Thomas F. Hickey of Rochester.[15]

It appeared that the Ukrainian Catholic Church
would now grow and develop without any serious hinder-
ances. That was not the case, however, for in spite
of the weakened Russian Orthodox activity among the
American Ukrainian Catholics there now began a Ukrainian Orthodox movement.[16] An important contributor to
the development and the spread of the movement was the
Transcarpathian priest Very Rev. Alexander Dzubay who,
apparently disappointed that he did not become one of

the administrators of the exarchy,[17] allowed himself
to be consecrated an Orthodox bishop in August 1916.[18]
As bishop, Dzubay ordained numerous priests with
doubtful qualifications. These events helped to de-
moralize the Ukrainian Catholic cantors[19] many of whom
now turned to Bishop Dzubay as a means of attaining
the priesthood without satisfying the usual pre-
requisites of that position. These new Orthodox
priests in turn tried to gain the support of their
Ukrainian Catholic friends as a means of gaining for
themselves the parishes to which their friends belonged.[20] Father Poniatishin was forced to publish
letters in certain localities to warn the people
against these machinations,[21] and he made personal
visits to distant colonies of Ukrainian Catholics to
prevent their falling unwittingly into Orthodoxy.[22]

As a result of the above developments
Poniatishin began to organize new parishes, even in
those areas where there were only a small number of
Ukrainian Catholic families. Not to do this, he felt,
would run the risk of having those families organized
into Orthodox congregations by the newly ordained
former cantors. Thus, during Poniatishin's administration twenty-four such small parishes were organized.[23] His zeal for founding new parishes to help
preserve the faith of the isolated Ukrainian families
did not diminish with the years.[24] In order to in-
sure that all these small congregations would receive
the frequent services of a Catholic priest,
Poniatishin formed a "Missionary Fund" in 1922 from
which the priests serving such small parishes might
receive necessary support, and from which funds might
be available to defend existing churches, by court
procedures if necessary. (A few of their churches,
according to Poniatishin, still remained in Orthodox
hands.)[25] Rev. Vladimir Lotowycz from Brooklyn, whom
Poniatishin appointed as treasurer of the Missionary
Fund Committee, was a great aid to Poniatishin in
putting his plan into effect.

2. Educational, Financial, and
Other Concerns

It must be kept in mind that during the entire
administration of Father Poniatishin there was a great
shortage of priests, and the added responsibility of
the newly organized parishes made the situation even
more serious. As a result of the First World War, and
finally due to the direct American participation in

41

that conflict, there was no longer any possibility of getting new priests from Europe, for "all ties with the dioceses of origin in Austro-Hungary were broken."[26] Thus, the second major concern of Poniatishin was education. The situation described by the late Bishop Ortynsky, that "the future of our Ruthenian people and Church in America lies in the school,"[27] was starkly real. With priests no longer arriving from Europe, the problem of educating future priests became more important than ever.

Since the arrival of the late Bishop, the seminarians had been trained in St. Mary's Seminary in Baltimore. The total number of seminarians (Ukrainian and Transcarpathian combined) in 1917 was ten. Of that number, according to their Spiritual Director, Rev. Joseph Dzendzera, only John Kolcun, George Chegin, and Yaroslav Skrotsky were studying theology, whereas John Taptich, Roman Kachmarsky, Stephen Sklepkovich, John Hundiak, George Simchak, John Zavala, and Michael Morris were still in the philosophy curriculum. In addition there were six candidates at the seminary's St. Charles College: Joseph Fetsko, Theodore Volkay, Nicholas Voloshuk, Andrew Rudakevich, John Loya, and Michael Rapach.[28]

Early in 1918, Father Poniatishin considered buying property in South Orange, New Jersey, for the establishment of a seminary affiliated with Seton Hall College.[29] However, according to church regulations the administrator cannot introduce any new policies. His administration is merely a transitional one. Consequently, after discussion of the matter with the Apostolic Delegate it was decided that it would be wiser to wait until a new bishop was appointed.[30] The matter was further complicated by the fact that the exarchy was administered by two administrators, and it was impossible to know whether in the future the exarchy would be united or split in two.

From time to time the few seminarians who completed their theological studies at St. Mary's in Baltimore, ar at other seminaries, were ordained to the priesthood by the Most Rev. Nykyta Budka, the Ukrainian bishop in Canada. Due to the extreme shortage of priests Poniatishin also accepted into the diocese several former Orthodox priests.[31] Despite these difficulties not a single church was lost during the entire time, according to Father Poniatishin, and, as already stated, twenty-four new churches were organized during the same period.[32]

The chief source of vocations for the priesthood
was the so-called "minor seminary" which Bishop
Ortynsky founded for the older orphanage boys. After
Ortynsky's death, Rev. Max Kinash, the pastor of the
cathedral, requested additional aid from Rev.
Poniatishin for the upkeep of the "minor seminary".
Finally in October 1916, at the suggestion of Rev.
Zachary Orun, the Ukrainian priests formed an Association of Sts. Peter and Paul, which was, among other
things, to concern itself with these minor seminarians. Thus from September 1917, all responsibility
for the boys in the newly styled St. Paul's Boys'
Missionary Institute passed to the priests' association and to a parallel association of laymen interested in aiding the missionary school.[33] The boys
attended St. Peter's school or St. Joseph's High
School in Philadelphia. All except three of the
twenty-seven students in this "minor seminary" were
orphans.[34]

Father Poniatishin was also greatly concerned
with the status of the parish evening schools in the
exarchy. With the exception of Philadelphia, where
the school was conducted by the Sisters of St. Basil
the Great, all the parish schools were directed by the
cantors. Considering the demoralization caused by the
activities of the dissident Bishop Dzubay, Poniatishin
gladly backed the cantors' interest in revitalizing
the Association of Cantors, which was originally
organized in 1914.[35] Among the goals of the association were such objectives as a unified system of
schools, school supervision, proper texts, qualified
candidates for cantors, and cantors' conferences.[36]
Obviously, such ideals, if put into practice, would
lead to improved parish schools.

A third major problem, according to the administrator, was the jumbled financial situation at the
Cathedral in Philadelphia.[37] Bishop Ortynsky had
decided to organize a Ruthenian Bank in Philadelphia
(chartered by the State on May 12, 1915),[38] and
savings of the parishioners were accepted. Some of
the money was invested in the buildings surrounding
the cathedral. When Ortynsky died the depositors
virtually made a run on the bank. Naturally there
were insufficient funds on hand to satisfy all the
depositors. However, the buildings could not be sold
because according to the bishop's will the properties

were to pass to his successor the new bishop. Thus
Father Poniatishin, although an administrator of the
exarchy, could not sell church property to repay the
depositors who demanded their money. In the end there
was no alternative except to ask Ortynsky's brother
Joseph, who was the beneficiary of the bishop's
$50,000 insurance policy for help.[39] Eventually the
bishop's brother turned over practically the entire
insurance account to repay the Philadelphia depositors
and thus saved the cathedral and other properties from
eventual court litigations.[40] The wording of the
bishop's will, unfortunately, added to the many difficulties for Father Poniatishin.[41] When he attempted
to get new loans or extend old ones, the banks, relying
on the bishop's testament, often did not want to recognize Poniatishin's signature. They demanded the
signature of a bishop.

It is obvious that internally, as well as ex-
ternally, Poniatishin's position was an extremely
complicated one. Discipline within the exarchy again
became more lax after the death of Bishop Ortynsky.
The administrator was forced to spend considerable
time and energy in curbing the autonomy of the church
committees, which frequently failed to appreciate that
the Church was to be administered by Church law. The
financial position of Poniatishin's administration was
further weakened because some parishes fell seriously
behind in the payment of the Cathedraticum which was
the major support of the exarchy.[42] In fact, it may
be stated that, many of the difficulties that Bishop
Bohachevsky was to face after his arrival in 1924 had
their roots in this period.

3. Special Problems Resulting from the War.

It has been indicated in the preceding chapter
that the American Ruthenians, cut off from their
European contacts by war, began in 1914 to form political organizations to help their native land and their
relatives suffering from the war.[43] Particularly
active in that respect were American Ukrainians who
originated from Austrian Galicia. Since Rev.
Poniatishin's administration was during the war years,
the years during which the Ukrainian problem came to
the foreground, the administrator did not shirk what
he felt was his responsibility. Consequently, the
church played a leading role in this important national and humanitarian work.

Shortly after the death of Bishop Ortynsky, the
Ukrainian clergy consolidated their efforts in behalf
of the distressed Ukrainians in Europe with a general
national organization called the Ukrainian Federation
of the United States. On October 10, 1916, however,
the Ukrainian clergy met in New York and resolved that
since, in their views, the Federation was carrying on
a narrow partisan policy detrimental both to the
Church and the people and since the political situation demanded the united efforts of all Ukrainians,
they would organize a Ukrainian Rada (council) for
that purpose.[44] At the same time the Soyuz, at its
annual convention held on October 9-11, also decided
to leave the Federation for similar reasons.[45] Thus,
on November 1, 1916, a committee of the Ukrainian
clergy met with delegates from the Soyuz, Providence
Association, and Zhoda Bratstv[46] and organized the
Ukrainian National Alliance, which was to carry out
the work decided upon by the All Ukrainian Congress of
October 30, 1915.[47]

It must be noted at this time that, upon becoming
the administrator of the Ukrainian part of the exarchy, Father Poniatishin took practical steps to end
successfully the misunderstanding that existed between the Church and the Soyuz since 1910.[48] The
renewed friendly relations between the Church and
Soyuz had excellent results in the humanitarian and
national political work of the American Ukrainians
during and after the war. The Ukrainian Alliance
(the Ukrainian National Committee from late 1918), was
an organization of political and humanitarian character that became the unofficial intermediary between
the Ukrainian national aspirations and the government
in Washington.[49] At the Alliance's first general convention, held on December 25-26, 1916, in New York,
the delegates representing the Ukrainian part of the
exarchy, the Soyuz, the Providence Association, and
Zhoda Bratstv elected Rev. Vladimir Dovhovich the
organization's first president.[50] The role of the
Alliance in publicizing the Ukrainian national aspirations and providing material aid to the victims of
war should not be under-estimated. A major part in
this work was played by the exarchy through its administrator, Father Poniatishin.

The greatest accomplishment of the Ukrainian
Alliance was its work leading to the proclamation of a
Ukrainian Day by President Wilson in 1917. Greatly
influenced by the fact that the Jews, Lithuanians,
and Armenians succeeded in obtaining a special

proclamation from the President in 1916, naming a
special day for the collection of funds in the United
States for each of these peoples suffering as a result
of the circumstances of the war, the Ukrainian Alliance decided in December of the same year to attempt
a similar proclamation for the Ukrainians. The responsibility for obtaining such a proclamation was
placed on the shoulders of the administrator, Rev.
Poniatishin.[51]

Together with the attorney for the exarchy,
William J. Kearns, Poniatishin discussed the problems
with Congressman James A. Hamill of New Jersey,[52] who
joined them in discussing the matter with the president's secretary, Joseph P. Tumulty, on January 4,
1917. The secretary made it clear that since similar
requests were being made by endless individuals and
groups, it would be impossible for the President to
make such proclamations in the future. The only possibility for such a proclamation by the President, he
suggested, would be an emergency resolution passed by
both houses of Congress unanimously. In spite of such
odds the officers of the Ukrainian Alliance went to
work on effecting such a resolution.

It is interesting to note that in preparing such
a resolution for Congress the question of terminology
became a major problem. Father Poniatishin and the
officers of the committee involved in the preparation
of the formal statement, held the opinion that the
text of the resolution must contain the term "Ukrainian", the proper name for their people. On the other
hand, Congressman Hamill, in whose Washington office
the resolution was being prepared on the morning of
January 24, called their attention to the fact that
the term "Ruthenian" could not be omitted from the
resolution, for he doubted if there were even a few
Congressmen who ever heard of a people called "Ukrainian". This fact had to be taken into consideration
by the framers of the resolution, aware that it had to
be passed unanimously. They finally decided to use
both terms in the text by incorporating the word
Ukrainian in parentheses after the word Ruthenian.
After much work by Poniatishin, his committee, Congressman Hamill, and others, to gain Congressional
support, the resolution was finally passed by the
Senate on February seventh,[53] and by the House on
February 22, 1917.[54] President Wilson approved the
Joint Resolution of Congress on March 2, 1917, and his
proclamation designating April 21, 1917, as Ukrainian

Day appeared on March 16, 1917.[55] The proclamation of
a Ukrainian Day by President Wilson was considered by
Ukrainian leaders to be their greatest accomplishment
since the beginning of Ukrainian immigration to America.[56] This was the first time that the name "Ukrainian" was used in a United States government document,[57] and the President's proclamation represented
an official public recognition by Congress and the
President that there was such a people as "Ukrainians"
in the world. From this time on the old name "Ruthenian" began to pass out of use in the United States and
the national name of "Ukrainian" began to take its
place in American usage.

At the same time that the Ukrainian Alliance was
carrying on its work to obtain a Ukrainian Day, serious efforts were being made by Father Poniatishin and
the Alliance to free Metropolitan Sheptytsky who was
exiled to Russia at the beginning of the War.
Poniatishin wrote to Congressman Hamill on December
27, 1916 requesting that the United States government
attempt to obtain Sheptytsky's release. In his letter
Poniatishin emphasized his need of the Metropolitan's
presence in the United States, and guaranteed to provide for his support as well as to bear the expense
for Sheptytsky's passage to the United States by way
of either Archangel or Norway.[58] Congressman Hamill
thought it wise to start action and together they
brought the matter to the attention of the State
Department. As a result, several cablegrams were
written to the American Ambassadors in Vienna and
Petrograd. With no replies forthcoming, Poniatishin
and Hamill visited Tumulty who, after a visit to the
President's office, informed them that if replies were
not received in three weeks the President would write
personally to the Tsar.[59] In the meantime the Russian
Revolution broke out, the Metropolitan was released
and thus American intervention in the matter ended.

After the armistice in November 1918, Rev.
Poniatishin and his colleagues felt that their com-
mittee had an opportunity to aid their people in
Europe by starting action in Washington towards
Washington's recognition of an independent Ukrainian
state. With the aid of Congressman Hamill,
Poniatishin was given an audience with Secretary of
State Robert Lansing regarding this matter. Obtaining
little satisfaction, the committee prepared a memoran-
dum to President Wilson, who headed the American Peace
Delegation in Paris.[60] After the American delegation

left for Paris, Congressman Hamill brought up a joint resolution in Congress on December 13, 1918, which if passed would have recommended that the American delegation apply Wilson's self-determination of nations principle to the Ukrainians.[61] Although the resolution did not pass, it did inform Congress about the hopes of the Ukrainians.

The Ukrainian Alliance (now reconstituted as the Ukrainian National Committee) also sent a delegation to the Peace Conference of Paris to aid the official Ukrainian delegation. The motive was to aid the Ukrainian cause by influencing the official American delegation headed by President Wilson. The failure of the Ukrainians to realize their political aspirations at the Paris Peace Conference also resulted in a loss of prestige for the Ukrainian National Committee in America. Thus, the committee was finally dissolved after nearly five years of important activity. Through its ties with similar organizations of other stateless peoples, its various deputations, memoranda, petitions, publications, and letters, the committee had publicized the Ukrainian aspirations before the American government and public.[62] Writing in 1934, Father Poniatishin stated that never before or since have American's of Ukrainian descent been so united and active in aiding the national organizations of their people in Europe. Through its work the committee gained great respect and influence not only in the American press, educational circles, humanitarian and political organizations, but also among the political and military leaders in Washington who turned to it as the spokesman and representative of Americans of Ukrainian descent for information regarding Ukrainian matters.[63] A major force behind this work was the Church. "The Church and the Soyuz," states Rev. Poniatishin, "actually created the Ukrainian national movement in America and educated the masses in it. Were it not for the Church and the Soyuz the greatest portion of our immigrants would have been scattered among Polish, Russian, Hungarian, and other churches and organizations, and would have been lost to the Ukrainian nation. They are two great fortresses of Ukrainian national consciousness in America."[64] In essence, Poniatishin felt that it was the result of the united efforts of the Church and Soyuz during the war years that Americans of Ukrainian descent began to understand that an appreciation of their national heritage was an important sign of cultural maturity.[65]

In October 1922, within a year after the disso-
lution of the Ukrainian National Committee, the United
Ukrainian Organizations of the United States was
founded under the inspiration of Dr. Luke Myshuga.
Rev. Leo Levitsky became the new organization's first
President. It continued the activities formerly carried on by the Alliance and its successor the National
Committee.[66] The Church continued to support the new
organization's efforts to aid the afflicted in Europe.
When the Allied Ambassador's Council finally decided
in March of 1923 that Eastern Galicia (Western
Ukraine) should remain part of Poland, all hopes of an
independent Ukraine were brought to an end. The results were felt among the Ukrainian immigrants in the
United States who fell into political apathy and
despair, a condition that was to be taken advantage of
by Bolshevik propaganda.[67] This propaganda in turn
helped to create new administrative difficulties for
Poniatishin.

4. Metropolitan Sheptytsky's
Second Visit to the Exarchy

The Ukrainians in Galicia faced grave hardships
following the great War. Metropolitan Sheptytsky
poignantly expressed the plight of his people in a
letter of December 18, 1920 to Father Poniatishin when
he wrote: "Our life is sorrow, gloom, silence, misery,
grief, - blood and tears."[68] Having received an invitation from Poniatishin to be a formal guest of the
exarchy, the Metropolitan made his second visit to the
United States in November of 1921 primarily to seek
relief for his distressed people. The Metropolitan
had two main objectives while in America. He wished
to collect funds for the war orphans in Galicia, and
he also hoped for an audience with President Warren
G. Harding, Secretary of Commerce Herbert C. Hoover,
and Secretary of State Charles E. Hughes, with whom
he wished to discuss the plight of the Ukrainians in
Galicia.[69]

Father Poniatishin made a special request that
collections be made in all the Ukrainian churches for
the war orphans and that they be mailed to the Metropolitan who was temporarily residing at the late
Bishop Ortynsky's residence in Philadelphia. On
January 30, 1922, the Metropolitan informed
Poniatishin by letter that he had already received a
total of $2,534.83 from forty-two of the parishes.[70]
Hardly a church failed to contribute to this

collection, with St. Joseph's in Frankford, Pennsylvania (whose pastor was Rev. Vladimir Petrivsky),
contributing $900.00, the highest amount on a percent-
age basis.[71] In addition, voluntary contributions
were made by the clergy. The Metropolitan also attempted to get financial aid from the Latin Catholics
during his visits to various members of the hierarchy
in whose territory Ukrainian Catholics and their
churches were located. However, due to post-war circumstances, aid from this quarter was hardly possible.
The American bishops were deluged with requests for
aid from various European nations devastated by war;
consequently, they just could not handle the situation. For example, Monsignor Michael J. Lavelle,
pastor of New York's St. Patrick's Cathedral and a
great friend of the Ukrainians, told Poniatishin so
many requests from Europe were received at the chancery that to satisfy them it would be necessary to
arrange collections for every Sunday for several
years in advance.[72] If the Metropolitan had arrived
during the war, or even a year earlier than he did,
the entire matter of aid would have appeared in a different light. In his recollections, written many
years after these events, Poniatishin hazarded the
opinion that upon leaving the United States the Metropolitan could not have had more than $15,000, from all
sources, for the Galician orphans.[73]

Shortly after his arrival, Metropolitan
Sheptytsky inquired about the possibility of an audience with Washington officials. To arrange an audience with the President, Poniatishin turned to friends
he had made in Washington during his work leading to
the Ukrainian Day proclamation in 1917. Eventually,
with the aid of Senator Frelinghuysen from New Jersey
and of President Harding's secretary, the Metropolitan, together with Poniatishin and the diocesan
attorney Kearns, got to speak with the President for
a few minutes prior to his weekly public reception.
During the brief audience the Metropolitan attempted
to inform the President about the harsh military occupation of Eastern Galicia by the Poles. Next the
Metropolitan wished to see Secretary Hoover, who had
been in Lviv in the Summer of that year as the American Relief Administrator. Again, Senator Frelinghuysen
arranged an audience. In the presence of Poniatishin
and attorney Kearns, the Metropolitan thanked Hoover,
in the name of the Ukrainian people, for the American
relief in Galicia. He then brought up the question of
the unfair treatment of the Ukrainian needy in the

distribution of the American relief packages by the
Polish occupational authorities as well as the general
political misfortune of the Ukrainians. When the
audience ended, the Metropolitan left Hoover's office
in a dejected mood for he realized, according to
Poniatishin, that his visit would not result in any
substantial improvement of conditions for Ukrainians
in Galicia.[74]

     In March of 1922 Metropolitan Sheptytsky left for
an extended tour of Ukrainian colonies in Brazil and
Argentina,[75] after which he returned to the United
States in August.[76] In October, when the Metropolitan
was convalescing from his serious illness in Chicago,
he requested Poniatishin to arrange an audience with
the Secretary of State, Hughes.[77] Again with the help
of Senator Frelinghuysen a meeting was arranged for
early November. Accompanying the Metropolitan to the
audience were Dr. Luke Myshuga (the representative of
the Western Ukrainian government in exile, who prepared a memorandum about the Polish occupation of
Eastern Galicia and her persecution of the Ukrainian
Church, clergy, etc.), and attorney Bohdan Pelekhovich.
After thanking the Secretary for America's hospital-
ity, the Metropolitan explained the reason for the
visit. He then asked for America's influential intervention at least in the matter of the persecuted
Ukrainian Church and clergy. The Secretary promised
to study the prepared memorandum carefully.[78]

     During his stay in the United States, both before
and after his sojourn to South America, Metropolitan
Sheptytsky naturally made many episcopal visitations
to churches, as well as visits to different Latin
Ordinaries,[79] and on September 4-8, 1922, he directed
a retreat for the priests of the exarchy at the Catholic Home in Bernardsville, New Jersey. The retreat
was attended by fifty-three Ukrainians and twenty-two
Transcarpathians.[80] In the evening of September 7,
after the last retreat services, the priests of both
administrations held a joint meeting, the first since
the death of Bishop Ortynsky, to discuss the problem
of filling the episcopal chair in Philadelphia. They
decided to send a telegram concerning this matter to
Rome. They also sent a delegation to the Metropolitan
urging him to use his influence in this matter when in
Rome.[81]

     Metropolitan Sheptytsky left New York on November
12, 1922,[82] returning to Canada from where, together

with Bishop Budka, he sailed for Europe two days
later. Although he did not succeed in his political
mission of obtaining aid for his people through the
intervention of the American government, no one could
have accomplished more. Sizeable funds were collected
for Ukrainian war orphans, and Sheptytsky's numerous
parish visitations provided him with first-hand
knowledge concerning the condition of the orphaned
Byzantine-Slavic Exarchy in the United States. At the
same time, the Metropolitan's extended visit naturally
buoyed up the spirits of the Ukrainian Catholics in
America. A few days after the Metropolitan left the
United States the Ukrainian newspaper America reported
optimistically that it was now a certainty that the
matter of a new bishop for the United States would
soon be decided.[83]

Upon his return to Europe, the Metropolitan reported on his observations in America at an audience
with Pope Pius XI. It was primarily through the influence and the recommendations of Metropolitan
Sheptytsky that finally in 1924, after countless letters and memoranda by both the Ukrainians and Transcarpathians for a bishop, the Byzantine-Slavic Church
in the United States obtained two bishops.[84] The
early administration of the new bishop for the Americans of Ukrainian descent will be the subject of our
next chapter.

CHAPTER IV

EARLY ADMINISTRATION OF BISHOP BOHACHEVSKY

1. Organization and Reaffirmation of Authority

The temporary division of the Byzantine-Slavic Church in the United States into administrative halves, following the death of Bishop Ortynsky in 1916, became permanent in 1924 when the Holy See decided to create separate exarchies out of each administration. Father Basil Takach, the Spiritual Director of the seminary in Uzhorod, Transcarpathia, was appointed bishop for the Rusyns, Slovaks, Hungarians, and Croats, from Hungary and Yugoslavia, who, since Bishop Ortynsky's death had been under the temporary administration of Very Rev. Gabriel Martyak. Bishop Takach's See was to be Homestead, Pennsylvania (suburb of Pittsburgh). At the same time, Father Constantine Bohachevsky, the Vicar General of the Peremyshl Diocese in Galicia, was appointed bishop for the Ukrainians from Galicia and Bukovina, who, since 1916, had been under the administration of Very Rev. Peter Poniatishin. Bishop Bohachevsky's See was to be Philadelphia, the seat of the late Bishop Ortynsky. At this time the Byzantine-Slavic Church in the United States was composed of a total of 299 churches and 231 priests. With the division into two separate exarchies, overlapping in territory, the exarchy for the Transcarpathians came to include 155 churches, 129 priests, and 288,390 faithful[1] and the Ukrainian exarchy 144 churches, 102 priests, and 237,495 members.[2] The history of the exarchy under the jurisdiction of Bishop Takach and his successors is outside the scope of this work.

Bishop Bohachevsky was born in the village of Manaiv, Galicia, on June 17, 1884. He completed his secondary schooling in Stry, and continued his philosophical and theological studies at the Universities of Lviv and Innsbruck. He was ordained in Lviv on January 31, 1909 by Metropolitan Sheptytsky, after which he was able to return to Innsbruck where in 1910 he attained his doctoral degree in Sacred Theology. Father Bohachevsky was a lecturer at the University of Lviv and prefect in the seminary when he obtained a leave to study the writings and lives of the Fathers

of the Eastern Church at the University of Munich.
During the war, he served as a Chaplain in the
Austrian Army at the Italian front. Following the
war, he held varied posts including that of Vice-
Rector of the seminary in Lviv, pastor of the cathe-
dral in Peremyshl, and professor at the seminary.
While pastor of the cathedral he was interned by the
Polish government for his work on behalf of the
Ukrainians and was freed only after the intervention
of the Papal Nuncio, who later was to become Pope Pius
XI.   Father Bohachevsky was Vicar General of the
Peremyshl Diocese when appointed, on May 20, 1924,
titular Bishop of Amisus and Ordinary for the Ukrain-
ians in the United States. Bishop-elect Bohachevsky
was consecrated in Rome on June 15, 1924 by the Most
Reverend Josaphat Kotsylovsky.[3]

Although news reached America in June 1924 that
two bishops were consecrated who were destined for the
United States, it was not until August 14, 1924 that
both bishops arrived. The two new Ordinaries were
welcomed at the pier by Bishop Budka from Canada,
Revs. Martyak and Poniatishin, and Monsignor Carroll,
representing Cardinal Hayes of New York, together with
numerous Ukrainian and Transcarpathian priests and
faithful.[4]   Both bishops were then escorted to New
York's Transcarpathian Church on 13th Street and then
to the Ukrainian Church on 7th Street for prayers of
Thanksgiving. A welcoming banquet was then held at
the Pennsylvania Hotel with Bishop Budka, seated between the newly arrived bishops, as the toastmaster.
The banquet was the occasion for the Ukrainian and
Transcarpathian clerical and lay leaders to express
their heartfelt greetings to their long-awaited
bishop.[5] On the following day Bishop Bohachevsky
left for Philadelphia, the seat of his diocese.[6]

The work of reorganizing a diocese, which for
eight and one half years lacked the leadership that
only a bishop could provide, required great energy and
determination. The strong will of the new bishop can
be discerned from the bishop's first pastoral letter
to his priests and fairhful.

My task is to serve God, to be concerned for the glory of God, for the
welfare of our Holy Catholic Church, and
for the salvation of the souls of the
flock entrusted to me. I desire to be a
good Shepherd, and a good Shepherd must

constantly have before his eyes the best
interests of his people, who have trans-
planted themselves to a new homeland where,
as in the old country, they must love and
serve God, for only then will they become
a great and glorious people.

Along with this, we can not be indif-
ferent to the fortunes of our homeland,
and, therefore, our efforts will be, with
your help Reverend Fathers and my beloved
faithful, to provide speedy aid to the
country of our origin.

Entrusting our common tasks that
await us to your prayers, my dear Fathers
and beloved faithful, I rejoice in the
hope that the Almighty God will bless you--
Brothers--and my undeserving person in our
undertaking for His glory, for the good of
our people, and for the salvation of our
souls.[7]

Bishop Bohachevsky turned his immediate attention
to the strengthening of clerical and lay discipline,
and to the re-establishment of church authority. The
Bishop reactivated the official church bulletin,
Eparkhiialni Visty,[8] beginning with the October 1924
issue; through it his official announcements could be
made known and educational and theological instructions could be passed down to the priests of the diocese. On November 12, 1924, Bohachevsky notified his
clergy that beginning in January 1925, the regulations of the Church Council of Lviv (1891), relative
to the competitive clerical examinations in theological subjects would be put into effect,[9] and in February of the following year he notified the clergy that
the appointment of priests to pastoral positions
would depend on the results of the examinations.[10] In
rapid succession, a whole series of directives dealing
with all phases of Ukrainian Church life in America
emanated from the Bishop's Chancery. The new bishop
lost little time, for example, in reminding the clergy
of the canonical regulations which prohibit pastors
from building churches, parish homes, schools, etc.,
without the explicit approval of the Bishop's Ordinariat. The pastors were informed that the Ordinariat
would demand strict compliance with those regulations.[11] Upon becoming aware of the limited Ukrainian
Catholic literature that was available in the United
States, Bohachevsky was prompt to suggest European,
and the few existent American publications, which he

felt would be useful to the clergy and the faithful.
Thus, for the priests he recommended, among others,
the clerical quarterly Bohoslovia from Galicia and the
monthly Dushpaster from Transcarpathia. For both the
faithful and the clergy, he recommended the Misionar,
published monthly within his own exarchy, as well as
another monthly with the same title from Galicia, and
also Holos Izbavytelia from Canada. For the children,
the bishop suggested the monthly Nash Priiatel from
Galicia.[12] In addition, Bishop Bohachevsky directed
the pastors to make every effort to ensure that the
parents send their children to Catholic schools,[13] and
he also called the pastor's attention to their responsibility to arrange for a mission each year in every
congregation under their care.[14] Nor did the vigorous
young bishop overlook worthy civic causes. For instance, he directed the pastors to celebrate memorial
services each year for the Ukrainians killed in the
War and to announce collections for Ukrainian war
invalids and orphans in Europe.[15] In fact, one cannot
read through the official Visty during the early years
of Bishop Bohachevsky's episcopate without being impressed with the energy with which the bishop attacked
the administrative problems he faced.

Bohachevsky's directives were at the same time
accompanied by important administrative appointments.
For instance: Very Rev. Stephen Vashchyshyn, pastor
in Frankford, Pennsylvania, was nominated Chancellor
of the exarchy effective September 1, 1924;[16] in the
Fall of 1926 Very Revs. Stephen Vashchyshyn, John
Kutsky, Anthony Lotowycz, John Ortynsky, Paul Procko,
Alexander Pyk, and Leo Chapelsky, were appointed the
Bishops Consultors;[17] while in the Spring of 1927,
Very Rev. Vashchyshyn, was appointed the Bishop's
Vicar General,[18] with Very Rev. Alexander Pyk, suc-
ceeding him as Chancellor.[19]

2. New Internal Stresses

Unfortunately, however, the 1920's were characterized by extremely serious internal conflicts among
the Americans of Ukrainian descent, which also affected religious matters. The bishop's hope, expressed in his first pastoral letter, "that the relationship established between us by the will of God, shall
grow progressively closer, and that you will feel an
even greater need to gather near the episcopal throne
and thus with united efforts we may strive towards
our common goal,"[20] was not immediately realized. On

the contrary, the early years of Bishop Bohachevsky's administration were characterized by an all-out struggle against the new bishop.

A brief historical summary of the conditions after the War is necessary for an understanding of the difficulties Bishop Bohachevsky faced after his arrival.

In accord with the general principles of the national minorities treaty concluded between the Allies and Poland in 1919, the Polish Diet approved a law for provincial self-government in 1922. This law, however, was not acted upon by the Polish government and the harassment of Ukrainians in Galicia continued unabated. The decision of the Allied Council of Ambassadors on March 15, 1923, that Galicia be permanently attached to Poland, was, therefore, a shocking blow to Ukrainian patriots. The Council's decision also affected the conditions among the American Ukrainians. Many Ukrainians fearing Polish rule left for the United States, thus creating in America the first purely political Ukrainian immigration. Some of these political exiles found it difficult to accommodate themselves to American conditions.

In the strictly religious sphere, prior to the War, the Ukrainian religious life in the United States centered almost exclusively in the Catholic Church. It has been pointed out, it will be recalled, that since the 1890's the Russian Orthodox Mission had considerable success in converting Ukrainian Catholics to Russian Orthodoxy. With the fall of the Tsarist regime, the Russian Orthodox Mission lost its material support from Petrograd, some of the Russian Orthodox priests who were of Ukrainian origin now tried to form their own Ukrainian Orthodox Diocese and obtain their own bishop. Some of the Ukrainian Catholic exiles went along with what they saw as a Ukrainian patriotic movement in exile. When on February 13, 1924, Archbishop John Teodorovich arrived from the Soviet Ukraine to become the first bishop of the American Ukrainian Orthodox Church he received substantial support from Ukrainian patriotic circles.[21] At the same time a movement developed among these patriotic circles that the people should control the Church. Since the leaders of the movement were also the leaders of the United Ukrainian Organizations of the United States, they were in an excellent position to propagate their views among the

Ukrainian communities. To win support, they began to
accuse the hierarchy of disloyalty to the idea of the
independence of Ukraine and for serving a foreign and
unfriendly political power. Thus, the Polish-Vatican
Concordat of February 1925, which normalized the religious relations in Poland, was brought to the foreground by the opponents of the Ukrainian Catholic
authority in the United States. The spark grew into a
great conflagration. "In practice," according to a
witness of these events, "this was a Ukrainian 'war of
everybody against everybody' which lasted ten full
years, and the effects of which are still being felt
by the present American-Ukrainian generation."[22]

The struggle against Bishop Bohachevsky which
began in 1925, produced a polemic literature of great
proportions. Dr. Luke Myshuga, editor of Svoboda led
the fight against the bishop, whereas, Dr. Osyp
Nazaruk, editor of America, strongly supported the
bishop. The conflict with the bishop had practical
effects on the Church and would have, if successful,
led to complete chaos.[23] The ludicrous attacks on
Bohachevsky--that he was a tool for Polish goals, that
he wanted to curtail if not stop all aid to the patriotic Ukrainian organizations in Europe, that he wished
to replace patriotic European priests with priests to
whom national interests would be foreign, etc.[24]--
appealed to many recent Ukrainian immigrants, who were
deeply disappointed with the failure of the Ukrainian
national movement in Europe. They became particularly
open to patriotic slogans, especially against Poland.
Even some of the priests became supporters of the opposition, thus contributing to the serious administrative problems of Bohachevsky. Some parishes denied
his authority and supported the opposition; others
were on the verge of becoming Orthodox.[25] Thus Bishop
Bohachevsky's energetic and often authoritarian attempts to reorganize his diocese and bring order and
discipline into the Ukrainian Church were attacked
and bitterly assaulted.

The struggle reached its peak in 1926-27, when
the opposition called for a Church Congress to be held
in December 1926. In his letters, sermons, and official announcements, Bohachevsky appealed to his
flock, warning them against the danger to their faith.
In the November 1926 issue of Visty, the priests were
officially put on notice by the bishop that he was not
convening a church gathering of any kind,[26] and a
regulation dated December 19, which was read in all th

churches, warned the faithful of the anti-church propaganda and of the organization of the so-called Church Congress. The regulation underscored the fact that according to Church Law there are no other church conventions except those called by duly authorized ecclesiastical representatives. It warned all the faithful against such an action and forbade them to take part in the proposed Congress and at the same time made it clear that in the event the regulations were disregarded that appropriate penalties would be placed on the guilty according to the Canons of the Church.[27]

The opposition Congress, attended by 130 delegates from 81 parishes,[28] met in Philadelphia on December 29, and organized an independent Ukrainian Greek-Catholic Church in the United States.[29] For cooperating in the preparation of the prohibited Congress or for participating in its decisions, at least three priests suffered suspension[30] and nine lay leaders who led in the fight against the Church or organized and participated in the illegal Congress were excommunicated.[31]

On January 23, 1927, in his sermon at the Cathedral, Bohachevsky publicly answered and refuted the charges against him and the church by the opposition.[32] The chief points that the bishop discussed were: the demands for a church charter which would place the control of the churches in the hands of the people, the complaint about abuses within the church, the opposition to the support of diocesan schools, and the hostility toward the Vatican-Polish Concordat.[33] From the very beginning the Concordat had evoked both strong opposition and strong support. The opposition held that it sold out the Ukrainian Church to the Poles, and the supporters insisted that actually it protected the Ukrainian Church in Poland and assured the clergy equality with the Polish clergy.[34]

3. Attempts to Improve the Bishop's Position

As the struggle raged about him, Bishop Bohachevsky continued in his attempt to bring order into the exarchy. In 1932, due to his efforts, the monks of St. Basil the Great (O.S.B.M.) were permanently established in the United States. Actually, since 1921 missionaries of this Order visited the United States from Canada and directed occasional missions and retreats in various parishes. In 1927

Bishop Bohachevsky agreed to have the Very Rev.
Epephanius Theodorovich, who was in the United States
while on route from Canada to Europe, remain in the
United States. Thus Father Theodorovich settled in
Philadelphia, where, with Bishop Bohachevsky's blessing, he began editing a newspaper entitled Katolytsky
Provid. Later Rev. Theodorovich moved to near-by
Chester, Pennsylvania, where he also carried on pastoral duties. On August 22, 1932, Revs. Sylvester
Zhuravetsky, and Andrew Trukh, arrived from Europe
and joined Rev. Theodorovich in Chester. Bishop
Bohachevsky, under whose jurisdiction the missionaries
were placed, felt that the Basilians should be primarily engaged in missionary rather than in parish work;
consequently, he suggested that they administer St.
Michael's Church in Hartford, Connecticut, which
served about one-hundred families. The Basilians,[35]
however, requested St. Nicholas Church in Chicago.
Thus, on October 1, 1932, the three Basilians arrived
in Chicago, with Very Rev. Theodorovich as the superior, Rev. Zhuravetsky as the pastor, and Rev. Trukh
as the missionary and director of the youth. In 1933
two additional Basilians arrived. The first to
arrive was Rev. Ambrose Senyshyn, (the subsequent
Ukrainian Archbishop-Metropolitan in the United
States), who was followed by the Rev. Maxim Markiw.
Shortly thereafter Father Trukh was transferred to
Canada, while the others remained in the United
States.

When the first Basilians arrived in Chicago,
America was still undergoing the financial crisis associated with the great depression; consequently, as
was the case with many other churches, St. Nicholas,
the largest Ukrainian church in the United States,
was in debt. With the added income from missions and
from their other energetic activities, together with
the considerable material offerings of their many
parishioners, the Basilians succeeded in paying off
the church debt. From their headquarters at St.
Nicholas in Chicago the Basilians, with the passage of
time, spread their work to other parishes in the
Ukrainian exarchy of the United States.

In 1929, Bishop Bohachevsky's position was improved, both in regard to his internal opposition as
well as in regard to the ordinary problems of inter-
rite relations, with the publication on March 1 of
the Papal decree Cum Data Fuerit,[36] which superseded
and slightly modified the decree Cum Episcopo of 1914.

The revised constitution defined more precisely the Byzantine-Slavic bishops' full powers of jurisdiction and helped to clarify the major practical problems that frequently resulted in inter-rite misunderstandings between the Latin and Byzantine clergy. For example: article 29 of the new constitution specifically stated "that attendance of Greek Ruthenians at Latin Rite Churches, even if it be continuous, does not effect a change of Rite." Furthermore, "in order to be transferred to another Rite, Greek Ruthenians must send a petition to the Apostolic Delegate," preferably through their own ordinary, "and set forth the true canonical reasons which seem to make such a transfer recommendable."[37] Article 30 states that "Latin Rite priests are not allowed to induce any Greek-Ruthenian to transfer to the Latin Rite contrary to, or aside from, the canonical provisions which govern the change of Rite."[38] Article 36 stipulates that "to avoid inconvenience which might accrue to Ruthenians, they are given permission to observe holy days and fasts according to the customs of the places in which they are staying; but such observance does not effect a change of Rite."[39]

The decree is equally specific on marriage regulations between the faithful of mixed rites. For instance, article 41 declares that "persons born in the United States of North America of parents of different Rites are to be baptized in the Rite of the Father."[40] Article 42 stipulates that "Baptism received in another Rite on account of grave necessity, --that is, when the child was near death, or was born at a place where, at the time of birth, his father's own pastor was not present--does not effect a change of Rite; and the priest who performed the baptism must forward a certificate of baptism to the proper pastor."[41]

Obviously these and other regulations were intended to protect the Byzantine rite Catholics from being swallowed up by the predominantly Latin rite character of Catholicism in the United States. There can be no doubt that Cum Data Fuerit contributed to a more cordial relationship between the Latin and Byzantine-Slavic rites in the United States, although individual instances of misunderstanding were by no means ended.

4. Education--Key to Growth of Exarchy

Despite the serious opposition to Bishop Bohachevsky and the disruptive consequences of that struggle among the Ukrainian Catholics,[42] which continued to the mid 1930's, the bishop energetically went ahead with the reorganization of his exarchy. The key to the reorganization and revival was to be education.

When Bishop Bohachevsky arrived in August 1924, not a single seminarian from the exarchy was in any of the Latin rite seminaries and the arrival of new priests from Europe had almost stopped completely.[43] Clearly, the training of young priests was of the utmost importance. Consequently, before the year came to an end Bohachevsky announced the reestablishment of the "minor seminary" or St. Paul's Boys' Missionary Institute, which had first been established by Bishop Ortynsky at 818 North Franklin Street, next to the bishop's residence. The "seminary" reopened on September 1, 1925, with Rev. Michael Kuzmak as its Rector. A total of 31 preparatory students from the first grade through high school were in the "minor seminary" that year. In addition three seminarians were now studying in Rome.[44] Obviously the two small homes at 816-818 North Franklin Street, even after remodeling, could serve only as a temporary location for the "seminary".[45] To Bohachevsky, the building of a seminary and a high school for the training of future priests was the most important immediate duty.[46]

The year 1925 also marked the opening of the first permanent day school by the Ukrainian Catholics in the United States.[47] The Sisters of St. Basil in conjunction with their orphanage in Philadelphia opened the school on September 8, 1925 at 702 Parish Street, with about seventy children divided into the first three classes.[48] Each year an additional class was to be added so that by the end of the fifth year a complete eight grade grammar school would be fully realized. The school, attended by the children of St. Basil's Orphanage and the children of the cathedral parishioners, graduated its first class of fifteen students in June of 1930. Although the school was originally called St. Joseph's School, the name was later changed to St. Basil's School at the request of Rt. Rev. Msgr. John J. Bonner, superintendant of

Catholic Schools, to prevent misunderstandings, since there were several St. Joseph's schools of the Latin rite in the City.

The early 1930's saw the fruition of the bishop's educational plans for his exarchy. In September of 1931, St. Basil's Academy for girls was opened by the Sisters of St. Basil the Great at their new Mother House in Fox Chase, Pennsylvania. A total of twelve students, most of whom were candidates for the sisterhood, were enrolled that year in the freshman and sophomore years of high school. The following year a third class was added, and in 1933-34 the addition of the senior grade completed a full four-year high school.

The announcement by the bishop's chancery in February of 1933 that a building had been purchased in Stamford, Connecticut, for a minor seminary and a high school for boys,[49] marked the beginning of the end of a long struggle for a major goal. The establishment of a minor seminary had been an important objective of the first bishop, Soter Ortynsky, and it was a serious problem with which Father Poniatishin wrestled during the difficult years of his administration. Finally, the goal was to be realized by Bishop Bohachevsky in 1933, nine years after his arrival in the United States. "In the last nine years our community has lived through a great spritual and intellectual crisis," wrote Bishop Bohachevsky. "It has become clear to us that the periodic outbreaks of conflicts, of everybody against everybody, among our immigrants, arise from the fact that we lack our own schools which would spread our culture."[50] The cultural importance of this project to Bohachevsky's administration is obvious. The broad significance of this event in the history of the Ukrainian Catholics in the United States was almost prophetically foreseen by _America_, in a welcoming article on the occasion of the forthcoming grand opening of the seminary and high school.

> Perhaps for once it will be possible for us to develop from within ourselves a sense of authority? Perhaps we will realize, that it is not for all of us to lead and stand at the head, but everyone must find for himself an appropriate place in the work of the people? . . .
> Perhaps from this very solemnity of

the opening of the school we will be
inspired to great deeds in the future?
. . .[51]

There is no doubt that the opening of the minor
seminary and high school in Stamford in 1933 ushered
in a new and brighter era in the history of the
Ukrainian Catholics in the United States. It marked
the beginning of the end of that long history of
struggles, of doubts, and uncertainties, concerning
the future of the Byzantine rite in America. The
American-Ukrainian Catholics could now look boldly
to the future. No wonder that the formal blessing
and opening of the Stamford institution was carried
out on a grand scale.

The festivities began during a continuous down-
pour on Labor Day, September 4, 1933, with the Most
Rev. Basil Ladyka, the Ukrainian bishop from Canada,
celebrating an open air Pontifical High Mass with
Bishop Bohachevsky and the Transcarpathian bishop,
Basil Takach, from Pittsburgh, presiding. The co-
celebrants of the Mass, which was held under the
rotunda at the entrance of the beautiful and regal
building situated on seven acres of the former Glen
Eden Estate, were Very Revs. Peter Poniatishin from
New York City and Philemon Tarnavsky from Chester,
Pennsylvania. A throng of about four thousand people,
including numerous clerical and civic dignitaries,
participated in this historic ceremony in Stamford.[52]

Thus, the "minor seminary" in Philadelphia was
transferred to Stamford, with the Very Rev. Paul
Procko, Rector of the seminary in Philadelphia since
1926, becoming the first Rector of the new Ukrainian
Catholic Seminary and its associated high school, the
St. Basil's Preparatory School. Classes began in
September of 1933 with twenty-two students. The following year the enrollment more than doubled. According to official statistics forty-five students were
enrolled for the 1934-1935 school year, with twenty-
eight of these being resident students.[53]

It must be added that in the same year the exarchy also had a total of seventeen seminarians
studying abroad, twelve of whom were in Rome, and five
in Stanislaviv, Galicia.[54] It should also be noted
that the great majority of both the diocesan seminarians abroad and the students in Stamford were supported by the exarchy.[55]

The growing enrollment in Stamford soon necessitated an expansion of the seminary and high school facilities. In July 1935 Bishop Bohachevsky acquired three additional buildings adjoining the seminary property[56] which provided a new classroom building, a gymnasium, and rooms for a library and museum. A Ukrainian Catholic Library and Museum, to be housed on the seminary grounds in Stamford, was planned early in 1933[57] and Very Rev. Leo Chapelsky was appointed shortly thereafter as the Director.[58] In addition, as early as 1935, Bohachevsky intended to expand the seminary institution in Stamford to include a college.[59] His plans were to create at the seminary a cultural center for Ukrainian Catholics in the United States.[60]

During the chaotic conditions of the mid-twenties some of the Ukrainian intellectuals in America were of the opinion that the Ukrainian immigrants were leaving their traditional churches mostly for cultural reasons.[61] Now in the mid-thirties Stamford was to become a Ukrainian Catholic cultural center where important religious and cultural events were to be held. Thus, for example, the seminary in Stamford became a frequent site of the yearly recollections of the clergy; it was the place of various conferences and celebrations, such as the Fiftieth Anniversary of the Ukrainian Catholic Church in the United States, which was held on Labor Day, 1934.

The opening of the seminary and high school in Stamford points up the educational and organizational goals of Bishop Bohachevsky in the 1930's. As a matter of fact, on the same day of the great festivities in Stamford in 1933, the third parochial day school in the Ukrainian exarchy was opened in Pittsburgh. (Only Philadelphia and Olyphant, Pennsylvania, had established day schools at an earlier date.) The hope was expressed at that time that perhaps the opening of the third day school on the same day as the opening of the first high school might serve as the beginning of a systematic organization of schools in the future.[62]

Bishop Bohachevsky's thorough organization of his exarchy and its continued growth since the middle 1930's, culminating in the erection of the First Byzantine-Slavic rite Province in the United States, will be the subject of chapter five.

CHAPTER V

THE ROAD TO MATURITY

1. Accomplishments to Second World War

Although the Ukrainian Catholics in the United
States had good cause in the mid 1930's to look boldly
to the future, the immediate outlook was still not too
bright. The internal frictions were not yet at an end
and, in addition, the Ukrainian Catholics were still
isolated to a deplorable degree from the overall life
of the Catholic Church in America. This was poignantly expressed by Rev. J. X. Heally of Boston, in
1935.

> . . . Here in our midst is an element,
> Greek in Rite, Roman in fealty, bat-
> tling unaided against the common enemies
> of us all, and we are hardly aware of
> its very existence. With naught but
> culpable ignorance to plead in defense
> of our aloofness, we extend no hand of
> fraternal greeting, offer no work of
> encouragement. Years of constant as-
> sociation have convinced me that of all
> the ills now afflicting our Catholic
> Ukrainians, there is not one which could
> not be rendered the more tolerable by
> our charitable cooperation. Hence I
> admit that their present lamentable
> plight is attributed in no small measure
> to indifference and lack of sympathy on
> the part of their fellow Catholics of
> the Latin Rite.[1]

These conditions were still common despite the
fact that Pope Pius XI, in his Encyclical Rerum
Orientialium, issued on September 8, 1928, insisted
on "charity toward those who, in the diversity of
rites, intimately adhere heart and soul to the Roman
Church and to the Vicar of Christ," and in which he
voiced his desire that "the first elements of the
Oriental questions" be taught in all theological
seminaries.[2] It is well to remember, however, that
the entire decade of the 1930's was a transitional one

for the American Ukrainian Catholics, a period during which such writers as Father Heally and others were making important contributions toward changing the unfortunate conditions referred to. Rev. Desmond A. Schmal, S.J., from Mundelein, Illinois, for instance, demonstrated a great understanding of the nature of the inter-rite frictions, and displayed a most charitable understanding of the grievances of the Eastern rite Catholics.

> The Ruthenians' grievance against us—and it is not without foundation—is that we fail to recognize in them true brethren in the faith; that we look askance at their rite; and that at times we fail to observe the very prescriptions of ecclesiastical law which are meant to safeguard them in their devotion to ancient customs and privileges which the Holy See urges them to preserve. Their grievance we can remove only by associating ourselves heart and soul with the Pope's sentiments toward the Oriental Catholics and by showing forth that association, practically, in our obedience to whatever the Church has prescribed for our dealings with them.[3]

The most serious obstacle to a spirit of fraternity between the Latin and Byzantine-Slavic rite priests was the fact that the majority of the latter at this time were married men. The reaffirmation of the old regulation (which had not always been enforced) against the immigration of married priests from Europe by the decree Cum Data Fuerit in 1929, and its strict enforcement, contributed greatly to the development of the spirit of fraternalism among the Latin and Byzantine-Slavic clergy. It helped to bring about a change in the character of the Byzantine Slavic clergy in the United States; from primarily a married clergy of European origin, to a celibate and American-born clergy. But it also resulted in dissention among the laity and clergy who saw in the decree a violation of the ancient rights of the Ruthenian (Uniate) Church.

Although Bishop Bohachevsky's enforcement of the celibacy rule resulted in a flare up of the fight against him, the great majority of the clergy gave their support to their bishop.[4] In the long run the celibacy rule meant a greater emphasis on the need of

an American-born Ukrainian clergy, which in turn, led
to a much improved inter-communication between the
Latin and the Byzantine-Slavic branches of the Catholic Church in the United States. With the flow of
married priests from Europe seriously restricted, a
native American source of future clerics was now in-
dispensable if the Church was to prosper in the future.
The reaffirmation of discipline and reorganization of
existing institutions, as well as the founding of new
ones, characterized Bohachevsky's administration in
the next decade and a half.

Thus in 1935, at the invitation of Bishop
Bochachevsky, Sister Servants of Mary Immaculate
(S.S.M.I.), arrived from Canada to establish a permanent residence in the exarchy. With Sister Servants
as well as the Basilian Sisters available to staff
parochial schools, Bohachevsky placed an even greater
emphasis on the organization of day schools.[5] By
September of 1940, the number of parish day schools
had jumped to sixteen, with seven of this number being
opened for the first time in 1940.[6] In 1937, the
Sister Servants opened their first Home for the Aged
in Philadelphia at Brown and Franklin Streets, and two
years later they established the St. Mary's Villa
Academy, a high school for girls, adjoining their convent in Sloatsburg, New York.

Beginning in 1937 frequent Eucharistic Congresses
were held within the exarchy.[7] The Congress held in
Chicago in June 1941, organized under the direction of
Very Rev. Ambrose Senyshyn, the superior of the
Basilians in Chicago, was an outstanding success and
attracted national attention to the Byzantine-Slavic
rite in America.[8] The Congress was attended by an
estimated 50,000 people. Among the notables in attendance were the Apostolic Delegate, Archbishop
Cicognani; Archbishop Stritch of Chicago and his
auxiliary, Bishop O'Brien; the four Byzantine-Slavic
rite Bishops in the new world (Ladyka, Takach, Buchko,
and Bohachevsky); and, of course, numerous clergy of
both rites.[9]

In addition to and parallel with the important
and effective organization taking place during this
period, there was also the continuation of some of the
difficulties resulting from the recent internal conflicts referred to in the preceding chapter.

For instance, the long struggle for the control

of St. Michael's Church in Woonsocket, Rhode Island, between the exarchy and the opposition claiming independence for that church, was to continue into 1938. After 11 years of disputation and court litigation, the Supreme Court of that state finally decided on January 25, 1938, that St. Michael's was to remain a Catholic church under jurisdiction of Bishop Bohachevsky.[10] The Court's decision was based on the fact that St. Michael's was a Catholic church under the jurisdiction of the Byzantine Catholic Bishop from the very beginning of its founding. Bohachevsky's administration considered this decision, and the motives behind it, extremely important to the continued progress of the exarchy.[11] Let us return, however, to our main theme.

Early in 1939, for more efficient administration, the exarchy was re-divided into the following seven deaneries extending over the entire United States: Scranton, with twenty-five communities included in the deanery; Pittsburgh, twenty-five communities; Philadelphia, twenty; New York, fourteen; New England, fourteen; Chicago, sixteen; and Buffalo with fifteen communities.[12] The Deans of the new deaneries were Very Revs. Nicholas Simenovich for Chicago; Anthony Lotowycz, New York; Alexander Rotko, New England; Michael Kuziw, Buffalo; Michael Oleksiw, Scranton; and Vladimir Ulianytsky for Philadelphia.[13]

In the Fall of 1939, a new high in Bishop Bohachevsky's educational drive was reached with the opening of a Ukrainian Catholic college, a drive which was to culminate in 1941 with the opening of St. Josaphat's Major Seminary. At a meeting of the bishop's consistory in Philadelphia on October 18, 1938, it was officially decided to found a college in Stamford, Connecticut.[14] Rev. Stephen Pobutsky, pastor of Auburn, New York, was named the director of the campaign toward that end. In March of 1939 a special legislative act of the State of Connecticut authorized the Ukrainian Catholic Seminary to conduct a college and to confer academic degrees.[15] Classes at the newly opened St. Basil's College began in September, 1939, with seventeen students enrolled.

2. Effects of the War on the Exarchy

The opening of hostilities in Europe on September 1, 1939, had an immediate effect on Bishop Bohachevsky's educational plans as well as on his exarchy in general, which depended on European seminaries for the training of its young priests. The war altered the plans of the bishop and forced him to hurry the long-intended opening of a major seminary.

In August of 1939, according to Bohachevsky's official explanation,[16] the first group of the exarchy's seminarians left for Europe and reached their destination in the first days of the War. In September, ten seminarians arrived in Stamford to prepare for their departure for St. Josaphat's College in Rome. Because of the hostilities the latter were refused permission to go abroad. Shortly thereafter, considerable funds were required for the return passage of thirty seminarians who were either in Rome or Innsbruck.[17] Thus, Bohachevsky, who had announced in a pastoral letter in January, 1940 his plans for purchasing substantial property in the vicinity of Philadelphia for the establishment of St. Josaphat's Major Seminary,[18] was forced by the circumstances of war to alter these plans.

The seminarians studying theology were sent to St. Mary's Latin rite Seminary in Baltimore, while those in philosophy attended St. Basil's College in Stamford. Finally in April of 1941 construction began on a new seminary building in Stamford to help accommodate the philosophy students. In the Fall of the same year St. Josaphat's Major Seminary for the diocesan theology students was opened in Washington, D. C. in a rented home on Lincoln Road, N. E., simply because the exarchy could not afford to buy or erect its own building.[19] The seminarians residing at St. Josaphat's attended nearby Catholic University. Thus after many years of planning, by two bishops and an administrator, the Philadelphia Exarchy succeeded in establishing its own major seminary, thereby completing the institutions for the training of its own clergy.

Another unusual after-effect of the war on the Ukrainian exarchy in America was the appointment of Bishop John Buchko, auxiliary of Metropolitan Sheptytsky of Galicia, as a temporary auxiliary to Bishop Bohachevsky. Bishop Buchko, who was in South America visiting Ukrainian colonies when the war started, was unable to return to Galicia due to the Soviet occupation of Eastern Poland. Early in 1940, in answer to Bohachevsky's request, the Holy See appointed Bishop Buchko as the auxiliary bishop for the

Ukrainian exarchy in the United States.[20] Bishop
Bohachevsky named his auxiliary the Vicar General of
the diocese as well as the pastor of St. George's
Church in New York City.

When early in 1942 Bishop Buchko returned to
Europe, to become the Apostolic Visitor to Ukrainian
refugees in Western Europe, Bohachevsky was again
left without an auxiliary. On July 6 of the same
year, however, Pope Pius XII appointed Very Rev.
Ambrose Senyshyn, O.S.B.M., as titular Bishop of Maina
and the new auxiliary to Bishop Bohachevsky. The far-
reaching significance of this permanent appointment
was readily understood by Bohachevsky's administration: to provide for continued episcopal authority
in the event of the unexpected death of the Ordinary.[21] The administration was mindful of the difficult period that followed the sudden death of
Bishop Ortynsky in 1916. Despite the efforts of the
administrator, during the eight and a half years that
the church remained without a bishop, the diocesan
debts grew and the authority of the church declined.
These conditions in turn contributed to the difficulties that Bishop Bohachevsky had to face during the
early years of his administration. Thus, the appointment of Bishop Senyshyn as the auxiliary loomed very
important.

Bishop-elect Senyshyn, who at the time of his
appointment was the superior of the Basilian Fathers
in Chicago, was born in Stary Sambir, Galicia, on
February 23, 1903.[22] After obtaining his primary
education in Stary Sambir he continued his secondary
education in St. Josaphat's Institute in Lviv. In
1923 he entered the Order of St. Basil the Great.
After completing his novitiate in Krekhov, he was sent
to Lavrov, Dobromyl, and Krystonopol, all in Galicia,
for his philosophical and theological studies. He was
ordained in Krekhov on August 23, 1931 by Bishop
Josaphat Kotsylovsky of Peremyshl. After a brief
period at Krestynopol, Father Senyshyn was assigned to
the Ukrainian Church of the Assumption of the Blessed
Virgin Mary in Warsaw. In 1933, he arrived in the
United States to join the Basilian community established at St. Nicholas Church in Chicago. He was
appointed Superior of the Chicago monastery in September, 1937, and it was under his direction that the
very successful Eucharistic Congress was held in
Chicago in June of 1941.

Bishop Senyshyn's consecration, the first in the Byzantine rite to be performed in the United States, was held in St. Nicholas' Church in Chicago on October 22, 1942, with Bishop Bohachevsky as the consecrator, and bishops Ladyka from Canada and Takach from the Transcarpathian exarchy of Pittsburgh as co-consecrators.[23] After his enthronement at the newly renovated cathedral in Philadelphia on December 17, 1942, the auxiliary established his residence in the administration building of the minor seminary in Stamford.

Because the Ukrainian press from Europe was made unavailable by the war, the press of the Ukrainian Catholic Exarchy in the United States was considered doubly important.[24] Consequently, early in 1940, a new weekly, The Way/Shlakh, began its publication. The Bishop's administration expressed the hope that the new paper, published both in Ukrainian and English, would find its way to the home of every parishioner within the exarchy.[25]

Naturally, the war had also direct and personal effects on individual Ukrainian Catholics, as it had on all citizens of the country. According to official church statistics, about 28,000 young men and women served in the military services up to about the middle of 1945.[26] Although the above figure is not final, it represents a substantial percentage of the official total church membership of 303,069 (men, women and children), as of 1945.[27]

Lastly, due to the consequences of the struggles in Eastern Europe, between two and three million Ukrainian refugees from Western and Eastern Ukraine, and other areas of Eastern Europe, were scattered through Germany and Austria alone at the end of the war in 1945.[28] Bishop Bohachevsky's exarchy attempted to provide material aid to these victims of war. For instance, on December 3, 1945, Bohachevsky mailed a check for nearly $5,000.00 to the Apostolic Delegate, for transmittal to the Pope, to be used for relief among Ukrainian war victims in the West.[29] Early in 1946, Bishops Bohachevsky and Senyshyn appealed to the State Department on behalf of Ukrainian refugees living in American occupied zones of Europe. An appeal for aid was also made to the American Catholic hierarchy, including personal visits by Bishop Senyshyn to Cardinal Alphonsus S. Stritch of Chicago and to Cardinal Edward Mooney of Detroit, both of whom

had shown considerable interest in the Eastern rite
Catholics within their territories. Shortly thereafter, a Ukrainian Catholic Committee for Refugees was
organized in Stamford under the direction of Bishop
Senyshyn. In August, 1946, the committee, which
worked in conjunction with the Catholic Relief Services of the National Catholic Welfare Conference,
sent Rev. John Stock as its representative to Europe,
where he carried on the committee's work for six
years. In his address, on November 13, 1952, in which
he expressed gratitude to the American Catholic Hierarchy for their aid in behalf of Ukrainian refugees,
Bishop Senyshyn stated that about 175 priests, over
300 orphans, and over 45,000 other displaced persons
had already been brought to the United States through
the efforts of his committee.[30] According to the
committee's representative at the N.C.W.C. War Relief
Services offices in New York City, who wrote in 1955,
100,000 Ukrainian immigrants left Europe for America,
and of that number close to 60,000 emigrated through
the mediation of the Ukrainian Catholic Committee for
Refugees.[31]

3. Wartime and Post-War Expansion

The Ukrainian Catholic Church in the United
States reached its maturity in the post World War II
period. Officially the Ukrainian Catholic Church in
Galicia ceased to exist in 1946 with the arrest of
the entire hierarchy and the forcible incorporation
of the church under the jurisdiction of the Russian
Orthodox Patriarchate of Moscow. The Ukrainian
Catholics in the new world now became the principal
source of spiritual and material leadership of that
branch of the Catholic Church. The growth of the
Ukrainian exarchy in America, and its role of leadership during the 1940's and 1950's will be the subject
of this section of our chapter.

The help that Bishop Bohachevsky received from
his new auxiliary was an important element in the
growth and expansion of the Ukrainian exarchy during
the period of 1942-1956. With Bohachevsky's blessing, Senyshyn took a very active part in various
national religious observances; such as, Church Unity
Octaves, Eucharistic Congresses, Conferences on
Eastern rites, etc. By celebrating Pontifical Masses
of the Byzantine-Slavic rite[32] and by delivering
addresses before these audiences, Bishop Senyshyn
further informed an ever-increasing American audience

74

about the Eastern rite Catholics in general and the Ukrainian Catholics in particular. Thus, the considerable isolation of the Ukrainian Catholic Church was replaced more rapidly by a greater spirit of fraternity between the Latin rite and the Ukrainian clergy in America.

Other activities of Bishop Senyshyn during this period were to benefit the faithful of the Ukrainian exarchy even more directly. The auxiliary, for example, made recordings of the Pontifical Mass, according to the Ukrainian usage; wrote and published missals and articles;[33] sponsored the painting of traditional Ukrainian ikons; etc., to help satisfy the needs of the faithful. He showed an interest in expanding the existing institutions and in establishing new church-related organizations as a means of fostering in the youth a greater appreciation of its Ukrainian Catholic religious tradition. He fostered, for instance, the expansion of the Ukrainian Catholic Youth League,[34] which had been originally organized in 1933 by Rev. Trukh, O.S.B.M.; organized the exarchical B.V.M. Congresses, the first of which was held in June, 1946, at Stamford; organized the exarchical Congresses of Altar Boys (Diocesan Acolyte Confraternity),[35] the first of which was held at Stamford in May, 1953.

The expansion of monastic communities and institutions was another phase in the growth of the exarchy in this period. In October 1944, the Missionary Sisters of Mother of God (M.S.M.G.) were established by Bishops Bohachevsky and Senyshyn, the latter becoming the guide and Spiritual Director of the new congregation. Under the guidance of the bishops, the sisters opened the Mother of God Academy, a high school for girls, in September of 1945 on West North Street in Stamford adjoining their Convent at Hubbard Avenue. To take charge of the household duties at the seminary in Stamford, and later at the major seminary in Washington and at the cathedral establishments in Philadelphia, the Sisters of the Sacred Heart (PP.OO.SS.CC.) were brought into the exarchy from Italy in 1948.

The Ukrainian Redemptorist Fathers (C.SS.R.) established a permanent residence in the United States in 1946 when, after many requests by Bishop Bohachevsky, they accepted the administration of St. John the Baptist Church in Newark, New Jersey. The

Redemptorists from Canada had been directing missions
in America for many years, now, from their center in
Newark, they would be in a much improved position to
continue and extend their work of missions and retreats for the clergy and the faithful of Bishop
Bohachevsky's diocese.[36]

The exarchy gained a third congregation of monks
to labor among the Ukrainian Catholics when in 1945,
at the request of the Holy See, the ground-work was
laid for the founding of a Franciscan unit for all the
peoples of the Byzantine-Slavic rite in America. With
the cooperation and support of Bishop Bohachevsky and
his auxiliary, the plan was soon realized. Rev.
Francis S. Duchala, the first American Latin rite
Franciscan to be commissioned to work on this project,
guided the first friary in Sybertsville, Pennsylvania,
from its founding in 1945 to 1948. Father Josaphat
(Emile) Ananevich, the co-organizer of the Ukrainian
Franciscan Sisters in Brazil in 1933, which were
introduced briefly into Bishop Bohachevsky's exarchy
in 1939,[37] was the first Ukrainian priest to join this
Byzantine-Slavic Franciscan community. In January of
1948, an independent Byzantine-Slavic rite Franciscan
Commissariat was established with Very Rev. Carol
Talariko, O.F.M. becoming the first Commissary Provincial. The headquarters of the new commissariat
were located at its second friary in New Canaan,
Connecticut.[38]

The growth of the Ukrainian Catholic Church in
the post-war period was also to be seen in the expansion of the existing institutions and organizations. For instance, by a decree of July 23, 1948,
an independent monastic Province of the Basilian
Fathers in the United States was created, with New
York being chosen as its headquarters.[39] The previous
year, 1947, marked an important development in St.
Basil's Orphanage, conducted by the Basilian Sisters.
After 35 years of operation in the crowded quarters of
North Seventh Street, the Sisters purchased eighteen
acres at 1825 West Lindley Avenue, in North Philadelphia, as a site for the orphanage. Although the
new grounds were partially occupied by a limited
number of orphans as early as 1948, due to extreme
shortage of funds it was not until June of 1953 that
ground was broken for the construction of one-fifth
of the original master-project, and it was late in
1954 that the new structure, containing the most
essential needs of the orphanage, was finally solemnly

blessed and dedicated. Thus the vision of Bishop Ortynsky to provide a spacious new orphanage on a farm in Chesapeake, Maryland, which was revived and revised after the arrival of Bishop Bohachevsky under the leadership of Very Rev. Mother Josaphat (who guided the Basilian Sisters for 25 years), finally came to fruition under the direction of her successors, Very Rev. Mothers Zenobia and Eusebia.[40] An interesting side note in the history of the orphanage is the fact that for several decades, since the 1920's, the orphans of St. Basil's were entertained twice a year by the Bishop Newman Council of the Knights of Columbus.

Pedagogically speaking, by 1949, twenty-five years after the arrival of Bishop Bohachevsky, the exarchy was to contain a very impressive list of institutions. For instance, besides the exarchy's St. Basil's College in Stamford, the Sisters of St. Basil opened Manor Junior College for women, adjoining their Mother House in Fox Chase, in 1947.[41] On the secondary level, five high schools were now functining within the exarchy. In addition to St. Basil's Preparatory School, the exarchy's high school in Stamford, the Basilian Fathers in New York opened St. George's High School for boys in 1946. Three high schools for girls were conducted by the various congregations of Sisters, namely: St. Basil's Academy in Fox Chase, conducted by the Basilian Sisters; the Mother of God Academy in Stamford, operated by the Missionary Sisters of Mother of God; and St. Mary's Villa Academy in Sloatsburg, New York, which was founded by the Sister Servants. In addition, twenty-five parochial day schools were now operating within the exarchy[42] under the direction of the sisters.

The exarchy's educational system was rounded out with the erection of a theological seminary building. In February of 1949, Bishop Bohachevsky announced that land had been purchased for that purpose in Washington, D.C., near Catholic University.[43] Although the bishop had hoped to erect the major seminary building in 1950,[44] it was not until May 31, 1952 that the new St. Josaphat's Seminary building was dedicated.[45] After long years of planning and striving, the Ukrainian Catholics had completed the necessary institutions for the training of their young priests.

The post-war period also witnessed major legal developments. The necessity of a revised and unified Code of Oriental Canon Law was apparent for many years.

To facilitate further smooth relations and church administration, Pope Pius XI formed a commission for the codification of Oriental Canon Law in 1929. With the promulgation of the first section of the Law, a steady flow of regulations emanated from Rome which affected the Ukrainian exarchy in America.

The first section of the Law, the motu proprio Crebrae Allatae, which contains the matrimonial law of the Oriental Church, was published on February 22, 1949 and went into legal force on May 2, of the same year.[46] This was followed by the motu proprio Sollicitudinem Nostram, the Law on Court Procedure, published on January 6, 1950 and becoming effective on January 6, 1951.[47] A third section, the motu proprio Postquam Apostolicis, the Law on Religious and on Church Property, was published on February 9, 1952 and went into force on November 21, 1952.[48] The Postquam Apostolicis contains a glossary of canonical terms including an enumeration of the following major Oriental rites: Alexandrian, Antiochan, Byzantine (Constantinople), Chaldean, and Armenian (Can. 303, Part 1).[49] The newest section of the Code, the motu proprio Cleri Sanctitati, the Law of Persons, was promulgated on June 2, 1957 and went into legal force on March 25, 1958.[50] It is this part of the Code, incidentally, which defines the hierarchical structure of the Church according to the traditions of the East.

Along with the publication of the new sections of the Law Code various new liturgical regulations emanated from Rome in the post-war period. The new regulations were strictly enforced by Bishop Bohachevsky. Beginning in 1949, for example, frequent topics of discussion at deanery meetings were concerned with the liturgical disposition of the churches according to the new rules.[51] In the official Eparkhiialni Visty, the priests were often reminded of the proper style and appointment of the church interiors according to the Ukrainian discipline of the Byzantine-Slavic rite. They were reminded, for instance, that the proper form of the altar was square, and that the tabernacle was to be small.[52] Whether it were in the use of the new Rubrics[53] or in the erection of Ikonastasis[54] (the screen with icons which separates the faithful from the sanctuary), the bishop stressed the new directives from Rome. One cannot read through the Visty, particularly from 1949 through 1952, without being impressed with the energy with which Bishop Bohachevsky enforced the new regulations. Issues

of the _Visty_ contain numerous and diverse directives,[55] ranging from theological questions to be
answered by the clergy[56] and inter-rite problems of
jurisdiction,[57] to the administration of church property[58] and exarchical honors and titles.[59]

The need for appropriate norms for the particular
conditions in which the Ukrainian Catholic Church
functioned in the United States had been felt from the
very beginning of the exarchy.[60] Starting in 1950,
particularly through discussions at deanery meetings,
the ground work was laid for the formal promulgation
of Temporary Diocesan Statutes which would become
effective throughout the exarchy. The first volume of
the Statutes was published in 1953, the fortieth anniversary of the exarchy.[61] This volume was a collection of eighty of the most important regulations of
the Ordinariat which regulated matters of Faith, Sac-
raments, Liturgical regulations, church discipline of
clergy and faithful, and the administration of church
property.[62]

The post-war period also marked the expansion of
the Ukrainian Catholic Church to the west coast with
the organization of the Nativity of the Blessed Virgin
Mary parish at Los Angeles in 1947. In addition, for
a more effective administration, early in 1950 a new
Cleveland Deanery was created when the Ohio parishes
were separated from the Pittsburgh district. Very
Rev. Dmytro Gresko of Cleveland, the Pittsburgh Dean,
now became dean of Cleveland and Very Rev. Ignatius
Halushka was named the administrator of the Pittsburgh
Deanery.[63] Early the following year a Shanokin Deanery was also created by dividing the Scranton district.
Very Rev. Vladimir Andrushkiw continued as the administrator of Scranton and Very Rev. Emile Sharanevych
was appointed the administrator of the newly created
Deanery of Shamokin.[64]

The expansion of Bishop Bohachevsky's exarchy in
the latter 1940's and the early 1950's was contributed to by the substantial new Ukrainian immigration
from European displaced persons camps. Many of these
immigrants came to America through the auspices of the
Ukrainian Catholic Committee for Refugees.[65] With
this substantial immigration there would be an even
greater need for additional priests within the exarchy.
The auxiliary, Bishop Senyshyn, showed a great interest in this matter and was responsible for signing
affidavits for 150 priests.[66] Consequently, about 175

displaced priests were accepted into the exarchy, particularly from the Archdiocese of Lviv and the Dioceses of Stanyslaviv and Peremyshl in Galicia,[67] which
were destroyed by the communist regimes. In 1946, for
instance, the greater part of the Ukrainian Catholic
Church in Galicia was forcibly placed under the jurisdiction of the Russian Orthodox Patriarchate of Moscow
after its entire hierarchy, including Metropolitan
Joseph Slipyj, were arrested and sentenced to hard
labor in Siberia.[68] Only Metropolitan Slipyj, whose
release was unexpectedly announced on February 9,
1963, has survived that ordeal.[69]

4. The Years of Fulfillment

In the eight years between 1953 and 1961, the
Ukrainian Catholic Church in America experienced a
series of important developments leading to the legal
maturity of the Church and her expansion to the present level. These developments began early in 1953
when Pope Pius XII named five priests of Bishop
Bohachevsky's exarchy as Papal Chamberlains, with the
title of Very Rev. Monsignors. The priests so honored were: Joseph Batza, Nicholas Babak, Joseph
Schmondiuk, Dmytro Gresko, and John Stock.[70] On April
5 of the following year, much to the gratification of
Ukrainian Catholics, the Pope raised Bishop
Bohachevsky to the dignity of Titular Archbishop of
Beroe.[71]

In October of 1954, Archbishop Bohachevsky's
exarchy sponsored a great National Eucharistic Marian
Congress of the Oriental Rites. The Congress was held
in Philadelphia on October 22-24, under the general
chairmanship of its organizer, Bishop Senyshyn, with
members of the Latin and Oriental Hierarchy in the
United States, Canada, Europe, and the Near East participating.[72] The highlight of the very successful
Congress, in the opinion of the writer and not neces-
sarily agreed to by Liturgists, was the concelebration of Divine Liturgies (Holy Masses) in different
rites at nine altars simultaneously, which took place
in Philadelphia's Convention Hall on October twenty-
third. The Apostolic Delegate, Archbishop Cicognani
presided at the unusual concelebration which was
witnessed by thousands of the faithful of the Latin
and the Oriental rites.

A great milestone was reached by the Ukrainian
Catholics in the United States on August 8, 1956 with

the establishment of a second exarchy for Americans of Ukrainian descent.[73] The new exarchy, with its seat in Stamford, Connecticut, comprised the New England states and the state of New York, which up to that time was under the jurisdiction of Archbishop Bohachevsky. Bishop Senyshyn, the auxiliary and Vicar General of Archbishop Bohachevsky, was named the first Ordinary (Exarch) of Stamford.[74] According to official statistics the new exarchy contained 101 priests serving 53 parishes (excluding chapels and missions), and a total Catholic population of 86,324.[75] Bishop Senyshyn named Very Rev. Msgr. John Stock the Chancellor of the new exarchy. Very Rev. Msgr. Nicholas Babak and Very Revs. Stephen Balandiuk, Basil Klos, Basil Seredowych, Peter Skrincosky, and Rev. Nicholas Wolensky were appointed the diocesan Consultors.[76] The new exarchy was divided into seven deaneries with the following Deans: Brooklyn Deanery, Very Rev. Vladimir Andrushkiw; Hartford, Very Rev. Stephen Balandiuk; Boston, Very Rev. Balandiuk (temporary administrator); New York, Very Rev. Basil Klos; Syracuse, Very Rev. Basil Seredowych; Buffalo, Very Rev. Alexander Styranka; Albany, Very Rev. Bohdan Voloshyn.[77]

With the separation of the New England states and the state of New York from the jurisdiction of Archbishop Bohachevsky, the Philadelphia Exarchy now contained 193 priests serving 122 parishes (excluding chapels and missions), and a total population of 219,720.[78] In addition, a partial administrative reorganization of the exarchy was also necessitated. For instance, a New Jersey Deanery was created by Bohachevsky, comprising the parishes of that state, which were previously part of the New York Deanery.[79] Most important, of course, was the appointment of a new auxiliary for the Philadelphia Exarchy. On July 20, 1956, the Holy See appointed Very Rev. Msgr. Joseph Schmondiuk, pastor of the Immaculate Conception Church in Hamtramck, Michigan, Titular Bishop of Zeugma and auxiliary to Archbishop Bohachevsky, who was soon to name his auxiliary the Vicar General of the diocese.[80] Finally, an Interdiocesan Council was created, composed of the Archbishop and the bishops of the Philadelphia and Stamford Ukrainian exarchies and Very Rev. Dr. Basil Makuch, who was named as the temporary Secretary.[81]

The new auxiliary to Bohachevsky, bishop-elect Schmondiuk was the first native born American of

Ukrainian descent to be named a Ukrainian Catholic
bishop.[82] He was born in Wall, Pennsylvania, August
6, 1912 and orphaned five years later when his parents,
Michael and Mary (Bocia) Schmondiuk, died in the in-
fluenza epidemic in 1917. Thus, he was reared at St.
Basil's Orphanage in Philadelphia. When Bishop
Ortynsky's so called "minor seminary" was reorganized
after Bishop Bohachevsky's arrival, young Joseph
Schmondiuk was one of the students attending eighth
grade. Upon completing St. Joseph High School in
Philadelphia he was sent to Rome for his philosoph-
ical and theological studies. He was ordained in Rome
on March 29, 1936 by the Most Rev. Alexander Stoyka,
Byzantine-Slavic Ordinary of Munkacs, Transcarpathia.
Upon his return to the United States Father Schmondiuk
held parish assignments in Aliquippa, Pennsylvania,
Rochester, New York and Passaic, New Jersey, prior to
his assignment in Hamtramck. On January 28, 1953 Pope
Pius XII raised Father Schmondiuk to the dignity of
Very Rev. Monsignor. Bishop-elect Schmondiuk was consecrated in Philadelphia on November 8, 1956, by Archbishop Bohachevsky, assisted by Bishop Senyshyn, and
Bishop Nicholas T. Elko of the Transcarpathian exarchy
of Pittsburgh.[83]

The appointment of the new bishop and the creation
of a new exarchy was indicative of the organizational
progress made by the Ukrainian Catholics in the United
States by the mid 1950's, as was the fact that now for
the first time Ukrainian Catholics in America were
obliged to follow a territorial parish membership.
With two or more Ukrainian parishes organized in many
cities, territorial membership became the obvious
solution. Thus, for example, in an announcement of
July 24, 1956, Archbishop Bohachevsky explained to his
clergy that now that the Church had completed her
organization and every parish had been allocated a
specific territory, the boundaries of which had been
publicly announced, the time for individual choosing
of parishes had come to an end and a territorial membership had become necessary. The faithful were
obliged to belong to that parish in whose territory
they lived. Should there be no parish in a particular
area, then jurisdiction over that region was to be
carried out by the pastor of the parish which was
nearest to that area.[84]

Obviously the Ukrainian Catholic Church in America
was reaching maturity. By 1957, fifty years since the
arrival of the first bishop and seventy-three years

since the beginning of organized religious life among the immigrants, a solid church organization had been established. In his Pastoral Letter of November 1, 1957, Archbishop Bohachevsky supplied us with an excellent summation of the substantial accomplishments of the Ukrainian Catholics in the United States.

> We have today 172 parishes and 11 missions, divided between two exarchies, not counting the separate exarchy for our brethren of the Pod-Carpathian regions. We have nearly 300 priests under the leadership of an archbishop and two bishops; rather than just one church, we have 223 churches and chapels. When we include in this three religious orders for men and the four religious orders and communities for women, two orphanages, three homes for the aged, the summer camp for youth, the major and minor seminaries, two colleges, four high schools, thirty all-day parochial schools, 256 classes of religious and catechetical instruction, the church choirs, the long line of religious brotherhoods and organizations, the Ukrainian Catholic Youth League, "Obnova," the Providence Association, the Catholic press and the publishing houses, then it becomes self-evident that the efforts of our clergy and faithful were not in vain. Our Ukrainian Catholic Church stands with a firm foot upon this land.[85]

The year 1958 was a climactic one for the Ukrainian Catholics in America. In July of that year their Church's growth cycle was fulfilled when the Papacy created for the American Ukrainians an independent Byzantine rite ecclesiastical province, with its center in Philadelphia.[86] The Ukrainian Church had progressed to a degree where a permanent ecclesiastical organization was proclaimed in place of the existing exarchies, which corresponded to the vicariates of the Latin rite.

By the Apostolic Constitution Apostolic Hanc,[87] of July 10, 1958, Pope Pius XII decreed a new ecclesiastical province comprising the Metropolitan See of Philadelphia (Archeparchy-Archdiocese) and the See of

Stamford (Eparchy), which until that time had been exarchies. By two Papal bulls, also dated July 10, the former exarchs were appointed eparchs of the new residential Sees. Thus Archbishop Bohachevsky became the first Metropolitan of the new ecclesiastical province with its seat in Philadelphia,[88] and Bishop Senyshyn was named the first resident bishop of the suffragan See of Stamford.[89] The solemn establishment of the Province and installation of its first Metropolitan took place on November 1, 1958 in Philadelphia's Convention Hall. The solemn rites were performed by the Apostolic Delegate, Archbishop Cicognani, in the presence of fifteen archbishops and bishops, over 300 priests, and over twelve thousand of the laity.[90]

The Papacy's publication of the major portions of the Law for the Oriental Church prompted Archbishop Bohachevsky to convene a diocesan synod to regulate such matters that were not specifically covered by the regulations of the Holy See and are therefore left to the jurisdiction of the local Ordinary.[91] Preparations for the proposed synod began in 1957 and in the Spring of 1958 the first section of the proposed statutes were being reviewed by the Very Reverend Consultors.[92] However, the work on the statutes was somewhat prolonged by the preparations for the solemn establishment of the new Byzantine Province and the installation of Archbishop Bohachevsky as its first Metropolitan, which was held on November 1, 1958. By the Spring of 1959, however, the projected new statutes which were prepared by Rev. Dr. Victor Pospishil, the archdiocesan canon law expert and the General Secretary of the forthcoming convocation, were mailed to all the clergy for their study and recommendations.[93] Finally, in his letter dated May 2, 1959, Metropolitan Bohachevsky notified all the clergy that the convocation would be held at the cathedral on October 7-8, 1959.[94] The convocation, promoted by the auxiliary Bishop Schmondiuk, was participated in by ninety-five priests of the archeparchy.[95] On October 8, Bohachevsky signed the Acts of the Convocation, thereby promulgating the 650 statutes which were to govern the Ukrainian Archeparchy of Philadelphia for the next ten years.

In 1960, to the gratification of Ukrainian Catholics in the United States, Pope John XXIII appointed Metropolitan Bohachevsky a member of the Pontifical Commission on Oriental Matters, one of the preparatory commissions for the Second Vatican Ecumenical Council.[96] Before that year ended the Ukrainian See in Philadelphia was again favored with the announcement from Rome that another of her priests, Rev. Victor Pospishil, had been named a Papal Chamberlain with the title of Very Rev. Monsignor.[97]

Suddenly, on January 6, 1961, the American Ukrainian Catholics were unexpectedly jolted out of their pleasant feeling of accomplishment and recognition with the grave news that their seventy-six year old Archbishop-Metropolitan had died. Metropolitan Bohachevsky's death closed an important phase in the history of the Ukrainian Church in America--a phase, extending over thirty-seven years of episcopal labor, during which the church was lifted from its near chaotic disorganization in the 1920's to full ecclesiastical organization with the establishment of an independent Province. An excerpt from a eulogy written by Bishop Senyshyn of Stamford aptly summarized the many faceted accomplisments of Archbishop Bohachevsky.

> When the late Metropolitan came to the United States, there were no seminaries, high schools or parochial schools. The number of clergy was small--not quite one hundred. With the help of God, Bishop Constantine initiated his many-faceted activities. He founded two seminaries; one in Stamford, Connecticut, the other in Washington, D.C. During his episcopacy there arose centers of learning: Saint Basil's Preparatory School and Saint Basil's College, Mother of God Academy at Stamford, Connecticut, academies for girls in Fox Chase, Pennsylvania, and Sloatsburg, New York, and a high school in Detroit, Michigan, and many parochial schools. In order to quicken missionary activity within the exarchy, the late Metropolitan invited the Basilian, Redemptorist, and Franciscan Orders. He favored the growth of the Basilian Sisters; he introduced the Sisters Servants of Mary Immaculate and the Little Worker Sisters of the Sacred Heart of Jesus and Mary. He was co-founder of the Missionary Sisters of the Mother of God at Stamford, Conn. He cared for the Ukrainian Catholic Press. He initiated

the magnificent Eucharistic Congresses of
Chicago in 1941 and Philadelphia in 1954.
Under his guidance various impressive
churches and schools were built. The
welfare of the people--especially the welfare of the youth--was foremost in his
heart. With his consent, the Ukrainian
Catholic Refugee Committee which sponsored
some 50,000 refugees was organized. He
sheltered hundreds of Ukrainian Catholic
priests. Briefly, under his guidance the
Apostolic Exarchate made great strides in
the fields of religion, scholarship, charity, and community life.[98]

The final funeral rites for the Metropolitan were
held in Philadelphia at the Immaculate Conception
Cathedral on January 17, 1961. The Apostolic Delegate, Archbishop Egidio Vagnozzi, presided at the
requiem services witnessed by 21 archbishops and
bishops, 25 monsignori, nearly 160 priests, civil
officials, and throngs of faithful. The Pontifical
Requiem Mass was celebrated by Metropolitan Maxim
Hermaniuk, the Ukrainian Archbishop of Winnipeg, assisted by the Very Rev. Basil Holowinsky and by Very
Rev. Msgr. Jaroslav Gabro.[99] Following the funeral
orations the Metropolitan's remains were laid to rest
in the cathedral crypt under the side altar of the
Blessed Virgin Mary.[100]

Metropolitan Bohachevsky's death was indeed a
shocking loss. Due to the strong ecclesiastical
organization for which he was primarily responsible,
however, the administration of the Philadelphia
Ukrainian Archeparchy continued smoothly. On January
9, 1961, the Very Rev. Consultors elected the auxiliary bishop, Joseph Schmondiuk, to be the administrator of the archeparchy.[101] Those who recalled the
difficult years following the death of Bishop
Ortynsky in 1916, however, anxiously awaited the permanent appointment by the Vatican. The announcement,
on August 14, 1961,[102] that Pope John XXIII named
Bishop Ambrose Senyshyn of Stamford as the second
Archbishop-Metropolitan of the Byzantine See of Philadelphia and Bishop Schmondiuk the second Ordinary
of the Stamford Eparchy, was therefore greeted with a
sigh of relief.

At the same time, much to the gratification of
the Ukrainian Catholics, Pope John created a third

eparchy and named a new bishop. By the Apostolic Constitution of July 14, 1961,[103] a new Eparchy of St. Nicholas in Chicago was formed out of the vast western territory of the Ukrainian Archeparchy of Philadelphia. It includes, in addition to the state of Michigan, all of the United States west of the line formed by the western boundaries of Ohio, Kentucky, Tennessee, and Mississippi.[104] As Ordinary of the newly proclaimed See, Pope John XXIII appointed Msgr. Jaroslav Gabro, pastor of the Assumption of B.V.M. Church in Perty Amboy, New Jersey.

Bishop-elect Gabro, the son of John and Catherine (Tymusz) Gabro, was born in Chicago on July 31, 1919.[105] After attending the elementary and secondary schools in Chicago, he continued his higher education at St. Procopius Seminary, Lisle, Illinois; St. Charles College, Cantonville, Maryland; and St. Basil's College, Stamford, Connecticut. His studies in theology were completed at St. Josaphat's Seminary and the Catholic University in Washington, D.C., whereupon he was ordained to the priesthood by Bishop Bohachevsky in Philadelphia on September 27, 1945. Since then Father Gabro served in parishes in Pennsylvania, Michigan, New York, and New Jersey. He also served the Philadelphia Archeparchy as a Consultor, a member of the Administrative Council, and since November 1958, as Dean of the New Jersey Deanery. On May 10, 1958, Pope Pius XII named Father Gabro a Papal Chamberlain, with the title of Very Rev. Monsignor. Bishop-elect Gabro was consecrated in Philadelphia on October 26, 1961, by Metropolitan Senyshyn, with Bishop Isidore Borecky of Toronto, Canada, and Bishop Schmondiuk of Stamford, as co-consecrators.[106]

The formal establishment of St. Nicholas Eparchy in Chicago and the enthronement of Bishop Gabro as the first Ordinary took place on December 12, 1961. The solemn rites were performed by the Apostolic Delegate, Archbishop Vagnozzi, at St. Nicholas Cathedral in the presence of fifteen bishops and abbots, civil officials, and numerous clergy and faithful.[107]

The official statistics of the new eparchy in Chicago indicate that it contained a total of thirty-nine priests serving thirty-one parishes (excluding missions), with a total Catholic population of 20,439.[108] In January 1962, Bishop Gabro announced the appointment of Very Rev. Walter Paska as Chancellor of the eparchy,[109] as well as a Consultor,

together with Very Rev. Dr. Stephen V. Knapp, Rev.
Michael Bochnewich and Peter Leskiw.[110] The vast
territory of St. Nicholas Eparchy was divided into
four deaneries and the following Deans were appointed:
Very Rev. Knapp, Chicago Deanery; Rev. Bochnewich,
Detroit Deanery; Rev. Leskiw, Northwest Deanery; and
Rev. John Lazar, Southwest Deanery.[111] On March 17,
1962, the four members of Bishop Gabro's consistory
were further honored by the Papacy when each was named
Papal Chamberlain, with the title of Very Rev. Monsignor.[112]

The formation of St. Nicholas Eparchy out of the
western territories of the Byzantine Archeparchy of
Philadelphia naturally affected the latter's size.
The official Directory now listed the Archeparchy of
Philadelphia as containing 141 priests serving ninety-
seven parishes (excluding 22 chapels and 3 missions),
with a total Catholic population of 160,912.[113]

Metropolitan Ambrose Senyshyn, who was solemnly
enthroned at the Immaculate Conception Cathedral on
October 26, 1961 by the Apostolic Delegate,[114] quickly
turned his attention to the administration of his new
See. On December 15, 1961 the Metropolitan See was
again honored when the Pope named Very Rev. Michael
Poloway, the acting chancellor of the archdiocese
since 1959, a Papal Chamberlain, with the title of
Very Rev. Monsignor.[115] The new Monsignor was named
chancellor by Metropolitan Senyshyn on February 5,
1962.[116]

In brief, the Ukrainian Catholic Church in the
United States had reached legal maturity in 1958 with
the creation of an independent ecclesiastical province. In January of 1961, the Ukrainian Catholics
were deeply saddened by the death of their first
Metropolitan who for more than a third of a century
had directed their church in America. In August of
the same year the official announcement that Bishop
Senyshyn of Stamford was named the second Ukrainian
Archbishop-Metropolitan of Philadelphia assured the
continuation of leadership in the new Province without serious delay. At the same time, the decision of
Pope John XXIII to create a new eparchy and name a
new bishop indicated that the growth process of the
Ukrainian Church in the United States had not ended,
and that new decisions and appointments would be
forthcoming when continued growth necessitated them.
Metropolitan Senyshyn attested to his own faith in

the future of the new Ukrainian ecclesiastical province when he publicly announced in a sermon on January 7, 1962, plans to build an imposing new cathedral for the Archeparchy of Philadelphia on North Franklin Street, close by the old cathedral site.[117]

CHAPTER VI

THE CONTEMPORARY PERIOD

1. Conflicts over the Patriarchate

There were, to be sure, problems facing the Ukrainian Catholic Church in the United States and its new Metropolitan in the 1960's. There was, for one thing, the problem of insufficient vocations to the priesthood, even though the Philadelphia Archeparchy had more seminarians than any other single Ukrainian diocese in the world. Among other concerns, the question of the use of the vernacular in the Liturgy, as well as the old issue of the Gregorian versus the Julian calendar, remained. But it was the issue of the erection of a Ukrainian Patriarchate, which was reopened at the Second Vatican Council (1962-1965), that was to lead to a great turmoil among the Ukrainian Catholics in America and bitter attacks upon Metropolitan Senyshyn. There are similarities between the difficulties experienced by the first Ukrainian bishop in the United States, Soter Ortynsky, during the years of his administration (1907-1916), those faced by the second bishop, Constantine Bohachevsky, in the 1920's and early 1930's, and those experienced by Metropolitan Senyshyn in the late 1960's and 1970's.[1]

The difficulties began after the proposal to create a Ukrainian Catholic Patriarchate was raised during the third session of the Vatican Council. The Decree on the Eastern Catholic Churches adopted by the Council on November 21, 1964 made clear the rights of the individual Eastern Catholic Churches. This decree clearly affirms the equal dignity of all the churches or rites and voices a strong concern for the preservation of the spiritual heritage of the Eastern Churches. Articles four and five, for instance, state:

> Means should be taken therefore in every
> part of the world for the protection and
> advancement of all the individual Churches
> ....

...the Churches of the East, as much as those of the West, have a full right and are in duty bound to rule themselves, each in accordance with its own established disciplines, since all these are praiseworthy from their venerable antiquity, more harmonious with the character of their faithful and more suited to the promotion of the good of souls.[2]

Thus Cardinal Slipyj and the Ukrainian Catholic bishops of the world convened a synod in Rome on September 29-October 4, 1969 and after their deliberations presented to Pope Paul VI a formal request for the establishment of a patriarchal system of government for their church. The Vatican's stand that a patriarchal form of government requires a definite geographical area (which the exiled Ukrainian Church does not have) appeared to many Ukrainians to be based not primarily on ecclesiastical but rather on political considerations.[3] The Vatican's position has led to a proliferation of pressure groups to fight for the Patriarchate. To paraphrase the view of a close observer, this battle has led to friction between Cardinal Slipyj and the Vatican, between the Cardinal and Ukrainian bishops, and has spread to parishes where it has divided priests and people.[4]

Serious demonstrations against ecclesiastical authority by members of patriarchal associations began in earnest during the celebration of the tenth anniversary of the founding of the Philadelphia Ukrainian Metropolitan See. On December 7, 1969 outside the magnificent new golden-domed Cathedral of the Immaculate Conception in Philadelphia, about 300 Ukrainian-Americans protested, in sleet and rain, the visit of Cardinal Maximilian de Furstenberg, prefect of the Sacred Congregation for Oriental Churches, who, together with Philadelphia's Cardinal Krol, presided at the tenth anniversary celebrations. The protest against Cardinal Furstenberg was, at the same time, a demonstration against Metropolitan Senyshyn, who had not participated in the Ukrainian bishop's synod in October and had not, at that time, signed the petition to the Pope for the establishment of a Patriarchate.[5]

The announcement, on February 22, 1971, by the Most Rev. Archbishop Luigi Raimondi, Apostolic Delegate to the United States, that Msgr. John Stock, chancellor of the Stamford Eparchy and pastor of St.

Michael's Church in Yonkers, New York, was appointed
auxiliary to Metropolitan Senyshyn by the Roman Curia,
without Cardinal Slipyj's knowledge, resulted in new
protests. Over a dozen Ukrainian leaders from America, including several patriarchal activists, met with
Slipyj, the principal exponent of patriarchal self-
government, in Rome on March 13, 1971 to discuss the
rights of the Ukrainian Church to select its future
bishops.[6] When on May 4 the Apostolic Delegate announced the appointment of a second auxiliary for
Metropolitan Senyshyn, in the person of Msgr. Basil
Losten, Senyshyn's secretary, the stage was set for
the most serious demonstrations up to that time.
About one thousand people gathered outside the Immaculate Conception Cathedral in Philadelphia prior to
the consecration of Msgrs. Stock and Losten on May 25,
1971 to voice their disagreement over the method of
nomination of two new bishops. To the accompanying
harassment of about 150 additional protestors inside
the cathedral, the two new auxiliaries for the Philadelphia Archeparchy were consecrated by Metropolitan
Senyshyn together with co-celebrants bishops Jaroslav
Gabro of Chicago and Michael J. Dudick of Passaic,
New Jersey, in the presence of Cardinal Krol of
Philadelphia, twenty bishops, over 200 priests and
sisters, and about two thousand faithful.[7]

Bishop John Stock, the son of Theodore and Mary
(Skrincosky) Stock, was born in Blackwood, Pennsylvania on July 5, 1918, and raised in St. Clair.
After passing through the local public schools he was
sent for his philosophical studies to the pontifical
university, Canisianum, at Innsbrook, Austria, by
Bishop Bohachevsky. Due to the outbreak of World War
II, he returned home and entered St. Mary's Seminary
in Baltimore, Maryland. In 1941, while residing at
the new Ukrainian St. Josaphat's Seminary in Washington, D. C., he continued his theological studies at
The Catholic University of America.

Bishop Stock was ordained to the priesthood by
Bishop Bohachevsky on December 4, 1943 in the old
Cathedral of the Immaculate Conception in Philadelphia.
During the next three years he served Ukrainian
parishes in Minneapolis and Chisolm, Minnesota, also
in Brooklyn and Yonkers, New York. In August 1946, he
was sent to Western Europe as the representative of
the Ukrainian Catholic Commiteee for Refugees, which
was headed by Bishop Senyshyn, auxiliary to
Bohachevsky. Upon his return to America in July

1952, Father Stock was named secretary to Bishop Senyshyn, and the following year he was elevated to the rank of Papal Chamberlain with the title of Very Rev. Monsignor. When the Stamford Ukrainian Eparchy was formed in 1956, Stock was named chancelor by its ordinary, Senyshyn, a position he held until his appointment as bishop. In December of 1962 he also assumed the pastorship of St. Michael's Church in New Haven, Connecticut. In 1966, he was honored again with the rank of Domestic Prelate and the title of Right Rev. Monsignor. In December of 1966 Stock was appointed pastor of St. Michael's Ukrainian Church in Yonkers, New York.

Bishop Basil Losten, the son of John and Julia (Petryshyn) Losten, was born on May 11, 1930 in Chesapeake City, Maryland. After attending the Immaculate Conception School in Elkton, Maryland and St. Basil's School in Philadelphia, he was accepted by the Ukrainian Catholic Seminary in Stamford, where he completed his high school studies at its St. Basil's Preparatory School and in 1953 earned his bachelor's degree from St. Basil's College. His theological studies were carried on at Catholic University in Washington, D. C., where he earned a masters degree in 1957.

Losten was ordained to the priesthood by Bishop Bohachevsky on June 10, 1957, and in the following year he was appointed a chancery secretary. Between 1958 and 1962 he served in several Ukrainian parishes in the Philadelphia area as administrator. In 1962 he was named secretary to Metropolitan Senyshyn. In 1964 Losten became a member of the archdiocesan Building Commission, and in 1966 he was named Comptroller and Consultor. In July of 1968 he was raised to the rank of Papal Chamberlain. He also became the President of Ascension Manor--a senior citizen's housing complex near the Ukrainian cathedral in Philadelphia--built by the Ukrainian Archdiocese in 1968 in conjunction with the government's redevelopment program. In 1969 Monsignor Losten was named head of the archdiocesan Bureau of Information and the executive director of the archdiocesan Insurance Commission.

Of the careers of these two new bishops one was destined to be tragically brief. Bishop John Stock, whom Metropolitan Senyshyn had named a Vicar General of the archeparchy and assigned as pastor of the

Annunciation of B.V.M. Church in Philadelphia, died in a tragic automobile accident on June 29, 1972. He was buried in the parish cemetery of Holy Trinity Church in St. Clair, Pennsylvania, the town where he was raised. Consequently, a mere thirteen months after the consecration of two auxiliaries for the Philadelphia Archeparchy, its ordinary, who was in relatively poor health, was left with one.

Since 1971, the conflict over the patriarchal system seems to have intensified. In the tension between the Ukrainian Catholics and the Vatican, some accuse the Roman Curia of neglecting the rights and welfare of the Ukrainian Catholics for the sake of its own diplomatic interests.[8] Various patriarchal organizations, such as the Society for the Patriarchal System in the Ukrainian Catholic Church, with its headquarters in Philadelphia, have sent countless letters, cables, and memoranda to Rome protesting the Vatican's refusal to recognize the canonical validity of the Ukrainian bishop's synods and their decisions.[9] Needless to say, among the Ukrainian Catholics there is strong opposition to having Cardinal Slipyj as Patriarch. In the minds of many, the admixture of church and fatherland poses a major problem. The friction among the American Ukrainian Catholics, therefore, is not really one between those for and those opposed to the patriarchal system. To paraphrase the closing statement of a perceptive author writing in December of 1970 about the unfortunately devisive character of the patriarchal movement: without a doubt, all of us are pulling for the patriarchate, except we're not pulling the same rope.[10]

Because of Metropolitan Senyshyn's failing health--he was suffering with diabetes for several years--the major administrative preparations for the archeparchy's participation in the forthcoming 41st International Eucharistic Congress to be held in Philadelphia August 1-8, 1976, fell upon his auxiliary, Bishop Losten. Losten, the Director of the Ukrainian program for the Congress, also became a member of the National Board of Governors for the Congress as a representative of the Eastern Churches. Rev. Martin A. Canavan, pastor of the Nativity of B.V.M. Church in Roxborough, Pennsylvania, was named by Losten the coordinator of the various Ukrainian exhibits, concerts, conferences, processions, etc. held during the Congress.[11] Msgr. Michael Federowich, pastor of the Annunciation of B.V.M. Church in Melrose

Park, Pennsylvania, Rev. Leon Mosko, Principal of St. Basil's Prep. School in Stamford, and Dr. Wasyl Lencyk, prepared a brochure on the Ukrainian Catholic Church which was made available to visitors to Congress events, and distributed at the Eastern rite Liturgy celebrated in Veterans Stadium on August 7. Part of the responses to the liturgy celebrated at Veterans Stadium were sung by a specially formed combined choir of nearly 300 voices from Ukrainian parishes in Pennsylvania, New Jersey, and New York under the direction of Osyp Lupan, director of the Immaculate Conception Cathedral Choir.

Due to the physical incapacity of the Metropolitan, on June 8, 1976, the Apostolic Delegate, Archbishop Jean Jadot, announced the appointment of Bishop Losten as the administrator of the Ukrainian Archdiocese in Philadelphia. Three months later, on September 11, 1976, after the illness which had incapacitated him for almost a year, Metropolitan Senyshyn died at the age of seventy-three.

Beginning on September 13, various requiem services took place in the Cathedral of the Immaculate Conception. In the evening of the fourteenth, for example, Metropolitan Mstyslav Skrypnyk of the Ukrainian Orthodox Church of the U.S.A., assisted by several of his clergy and the choir of St. Vladimir's Orthodox Cathedral, celebrated a Panachyda, a requiem service for the dead. Leading hundreds of clergy of various rites in the funeral services on the sixteenth, was Cardinal Joseph Slipyj, who arrived from Rome the previous evening. The Requiem Liturgy was celebrated by eleven members of the hierarchy, headed by Cardinal Slipyj, Metropolitan Maxim Hermaniuk from Winnipeg, Canada, and Metropolitan Stephen Kocisko of Pittsburgh (Munhall).[12] Attending the Liturgy were Cardinal John Krol of Philadelphia; Frank Rizzo, the Mayor of Philadelphia, Metropolitan Skrypnyk of the Ukrainian Orthodox Church; Dr. Myron Kuropas, President Gerald Ford's personal representative; numerous bishops, clergy, sisters, and thousands of the faithful. It seems fitting that Metropolitan Senyshyn was laid to rest, on September 16, in the crypt of the lower church of the magnificent Immaculate Conception Cathedral which he had built less than a decade earlier.

After officiating at Senyshyn's funeral rites in September, 1976, Cardinal Slipyj made an extensive

tour of the United States and Canada. On September
eighteenth he met with President Gerald Ford at the
White House, accompanied by Bishop Losten and several
other leaders of the Ukrainian community.[13] While in
Washington, Slipyj visited President Kennedy's grave
in Arlington National Cemetery, where a service for
the dead was celebrated. Prior to his departure for
Canada early in October he also made visits to cities
such as New York, Jersey City and Passaic in New
Jersey, Chicago, and Cleveland, Ohio, all of which
have major Ukrainian organizations and institutions.
Because the Cardinal is the central figure in the
struggle for a Patriarchate, his extended sojourn in
the United States tended, in part, to fan the current
turbulence among the Ukrainian Catholics in America.
For example, the news that Cardinal Slipyj agreed to
bless a site for a church not authorized by the archeparchy resulted in an official complaint by Bishop
Losten, administrator of the Philadelphia Archeparchy, to Cardinal Slipyj (September 20, 1976).[14]
In addition, several priests involved in the creation
of independent parishes in Philadelphia and Cleveland,
Ohio, were suspended by the administrator as a result
of their actions.[15]

2. Metropolitan Senyshyn's Period in Review

We have previously discussed Metropolitan
Senyshyn's many contributions as an auxiliary to
Bohachevsky and as ordinary of Stamford.[16] His work
for the Ukrainian Catholic Church in America, and for
Ukrainians in general, did not slacken after he became
Metropolitan in 1961. Senyshyn's concern, for example,
over the fate of the "silent church" in the Ukraine is
suggested by his annual addresses over The Voice of
America during the Christmas and Easter seasons. On
the occasion of Slipyj's seventieth anniversary in
1962, Senyshyn held a press conference and published
a brochure informing Americans about Slipyj's suffering in defense of his church and people.[17] During the
World Synod of Bishops in 1971, Senyshyn and his fellow
Ukrainian American bishops issued a memorandum concerning the suffering church in the Ukraine.
Senyshyn's concerns were not limited, of course, to
strictly religious matters. During his audience with
Pope Paul on October 28, 1974, for instance, Metropolitan Senyshyn requested the Pope to intercede in
the case of imprisoned Ukrainian dissident historian,
Valentyn Moroz. He made similar appeals for Moroz
and cybernetics specialist, Leonid Plyushch, to

97

President Ford and to all the Catholic bishops in the United States requesting them to intercede in behalf of imprisoned Ukrainian dissidents.[18]

The turbulence among the Ukrainian Catholics in the United States during the last dozen years should not overshadow the accomplishments of the Ukrainian Church in America during the fifteen years that Senyshyn was Metropolitan. In the Philadelphia Archeparchy alone, twenty-five new churches were built and eight new parishes and missions were established.[19] In 1965 Senyshyn established two new cultural institutions, the Ukrainian Studies Center and the Byzantine Slavic Arts Foundation, both of which are located at St. Josephat's Seminary in Washington, D. C. In 1973 the Archeparchy was honored when its Metropolitan was appointed a member of the Sacred Congregation for the Eastern Churches by Pope Paul, and again in 1975 when one of its priests, Msgr. Dr. Walter Paska, now rector of St. Josephat's Seminary and lecturer in the Department of Canon Law at The Catholic University of America, was appointed a consultor to the Pontifical Commission for the Revision of the Code of Oriental Law.[20] Late in 1974 Metropolitan Senyshyn gave his approval for the establishment of a League of Ukrainian Catholic Youth for young adults, which was organized early in 1976 as a branch of the League of Ukrainian Catholics. In the Summer of 1976 plans were instituted for the Second Archeparchal Convocation which was held in the Fall of 1978.[21]

The archeparchy has also been a vital participant in the redevelopment of the East Poplar Renewal Area in Philadelphia, which extends from ninth to fifth street and from Girard Avenue to Spring Garden Street. In addition to the monumental new cathedral which, with its huge golden dome, has become a Philadelphia landmark since its construction in 1966, the archeparchy has built in the area a school, hall, and gymnasium, a child care center, and a housing unit for senior citizens--Ascension Manor. In Washington, D. C., the Holy Family Parish of the archeparchy has been developing plans since 1975 to erect a new memorial church, a grotto, and a commemorative cross to honor the 1000th anniversary of Christianity in the Ukraine, to be constructed on a three acre site near St. Josaphat's Seminary.

Impressive programs and construction projects

were also under way during this period in the suffragan sees of Stamford and Chicago. In the Stamford Eparchy, for example, at Saint Basil College, a new dormitory-classroom building, a project begun by Senyshyn when he was the ordinary in Stamford, was completed by his successor, Bishop Schmondiuk. In the attempt to aid the Ukrainian missionary church in South America, Schmondiuk encouraged the parishes of his diocese to adopt missionary parishes in Argentina.[22] In September, 1976, Bishop Schmondiuk formally blessed the imposing commemorative cross erected at the Holy Spirit Cemetery in Hamptonburgh, New York, which the bishop had purchased and developed for the Stamford Diocese in 1971. After a multi-year campaign for funds, the eparchy's St. George's Church on Seventh Street between Second and Third Avenues in lower Manhattan began the construction of a new three million dollar church in the Spring of 1976.

The Eparchy of St. Nicholas in Chicago which was created in 1961, the year Bishop Senyshyn became Metropolitan, also witnessed important developments during the sixties and the seventies. Its ordinary, Bishop Gabro, was the first Ukrainian bishop in the United States who was wholly a product of American schools. Among the institutions introduced into the new diocese by Gabro was a diocesan newspaper, The New Star, and the St. Athanasius Ecumenical Center. In 1972 he established the Christ Child Center, a mission station in Nazareth, Israel, which the Chicago Eparchy supports, and in 1976 a mission was also started in Hawaii, which is within the limits of the eparchy.[23] Late in the Summer of 1974 work began on the extensive two million dollar restoration of the beautiful old St. Nicholas Cathedral (originally built in 1913-1915), which was completed in 1977.[24] In 1975, the eparchy's St. Joseph's parish in Chicago began the construction of the unique, new, thirteen domed, circular St. Joseph's Church which was also completed in 1977.

Rounding out Archbishop Senyshyn's period as a Metropolitan, it is to be noted that, according to a comparative study made in 1976, the United States had the largest Ukrainian Catholic population, numbering 284,552 persons, out of a total of 874,881 Ukrainian Catholics in the free world. Since the future of the American Ukrainian Catholic Church obviously rests on the continued flow of the young into its membership, it is of interest that the study also indicates that there were 1,323 baptisms in the 206 parishes that made up the Ukrainian Church in America in 1976.[25] Furthermore, in 1977 this church operated thirty-one elementary schools, eleven high schools, and three colleges, with a combined enrollment of 6,352 students.[26]

3. Church Leadership in Flux

During the interim between the death of Metropolitan Senyshyn and the appointment and installation of his successor, the archeparchy remained under the administration of Bishop Losten. Among the developments during that period, the following deserve mention: 1) Although many honors and titles have been bestowed upon priests of the archeparchy in recent years, (such as Canon, Mitred Priest, Archpriest, Mitred Archpriest, etc.), the highest honorary title for a priest in the Ukrainian Church, that of a Mitred Prelate (Archimandrite) was conferred upon two priests of the archeparchy in October 1976 by Cardinal Slipyj at the request of Bishop Losten.[27] The two priests so honored were Msgr. Dr. Victor J. Pospishil, pastor of St. Mary's Church, Carteret, New Jersey, canon lawyer and presiding judge of the Archeparchal Court, as well as former professor at Manhattan College; and Msgr. Dr. Basil Makuch, historian and former Rector of St. Josaphat's Seminary in Washington, D. C. 2) On April 25, Bishop Losten presided at the formal ground-breaking for the 140 new housing units of Ascension Manor II at 970 North Seventh Street, the archeparchy's newest addition to the East Poplar Renewal Area in Philadelphia. 3) The first meeting of the newly-formed Priest's Senate of the archeparchy was held in Philadelphia on May 10. The fifteen member consultative body, to aid in the administration of the archeparchy, elected Rev. Dr. Ronald P. Popivchak, pastor of SS. Peter and Paul's Church in Bridgeport, Pa., President of the Senate; Msgr. Stephen Sulyk, pastor of the Assumption of the B.V.M. Church in Perth Amboy, New Jersey, Vice President; and Rev. Martin A. Canavan, from Roxborough's Nativity Church, Secretary. 4) On May 22, Bishop Losten officiated at the groundbreaking for the first phase of the construction of the proposed Holy Family Shrine in Washington, D. C.

On October 1, 1977, the Papal Delegate, Archbishop Jadot, announced that Pope Paul VI had named

Bishop Joseph M. Schmondiuk of Stamford, as the new Archbishop of the Philadelphia Archeparchy and the Metropolitan of the Ukrainian Catholics in America. At the same time, Archbishop Jadot reported that the administrator of the archeparchy, Bishop Losten, had been appointed the new ordinary of the Stamford Eparchy.

Archbishop Schmondiuk, the third Metropolitan for the Ukrainian Catholics in the United States and the first to be born in America, was formally installed by the Apostolic Delegate at the Cathedral of the Immaculate Conception in Philadelphia on December 1. The installation ceremony was followed by a Pontifical Liturgy concelebrated by Metropolitan Schmondiuk, the Ukrainian Metropolitan of Canada, Archbishop Hermaniuk of Winnipeg, seven Ukrainian bishops from the United States and Canada, and other church dignitaries of the American Ukrainian Catholic Church.[28] More than 2,000 people attended the impressive ceremonies. Among the honored guests were: Cardinal Krol of Philadelphia; Cardinal William Baum of Washington, D. C.; Metropolitan Joseph Kocisko, of the Transcarpathian Archeparchy of Pittsburgh; 26 Latin rite bishops; four Transcarpathian bishops; Philadelphia's mayor, Frank Rizzo; and representatives of numerous Ukrainian organizations and institutions, including members of Ukrainian Orthodox and Evangelical church groups.

Metropolitan Schmondiuk installed Bishop Losten as the third Eparch of Stamford at the seminary chapel in Stamford, on December 7, in the presence of the Papal Delegate, Archbishop Jadot; Archbishop Joseph Tawil of Newton, Massachusetts, head of the Melkite-rite Catholic Church in America; Archbishop John F. Whealon of Hartford, Connecticut; eleven Latin rite bishops; numerous priests and sisters; representatives of various Ukrainian organizations and institutions; and hundreds of the faithful. Concelebrating the Pontifical Liturgy with the newly-installed bishop were: Metropolitans Schmondiuk, Hermaniuk, and Kocisko; five Ukrainian and Transcarpathian bishops; and other dignitaries of the Ukrainian Catholic Church in America.[29] Because of the limited space in the seminary chapel, many of the more than 900 attending the colorful ceremonies had to be accommodated in adjoining rooms where they watched the installation ceremonies on television screens.

Thus, after a year's interregnum the American

Ukrainian Catholics once again had a Metropolitan to head their Church. They were stunned, however, when Archbishop Schmondiuk died suddenly on Christmas day in 1978, following a massive heart attack. In the span of twenty-seven months the Ukrainian Catholic Church in America lost two Metropolitans.

The Requiem Liturgy for Archbishop Schmondiuk was held on December 30 at the Immaculate Conception Cathedral in Philadelphia. Metropolitans Hermaniuk of Winnipeg and Kocisko of Pittsburgh were the main celebrants, assisted by ten Ukrainian and Trans-carpathian bishops. The Latin rite was represented by Cardinal Krol of Philadelphia and five additional bishops. Also present were representatives of the Ukrainian and Greek Orthodox Churches, numerous priests and sisters, city officials, and about fifteen hundred of the faithful.[30] Following the funeral Mass the Archbishop's body was transported for burial to the Ukrainian Catholic Cemetery of the Holy Spirit in Hamptonburgh, New York which the Archbishop had earlier established for the Ukrainian Diocese of Stamford while he was its bishop.

Msgr. Stephen Chehansky, Vicar General under Archbishop Schmondiuk and pastor of St. John the Baptist Church in Northampton, Pa., was selected by the archdiocesan consultors as the administrator of the See until the appointment of a new spiritual leader for the Ukrainian Catholics in the United States.

Nearly nine months elapsed when the Apostolic Delegate, Archbishop Jadot, announced on September 21, 1979 that Pope John Paul II had appointed Msgr. Myroslav Lubachivsky, at the time the Spiritual Direc-tor of St. Basil's Seminary in Stamford, as the new Archbishop-Metropolitan for the American Ukrainian Catholics. The appointment evoked numerous reports that Cardinal Slipyj and some of the Ukrainian bishops, as well as other Ukrainian Catholics, were upset about the lack of consultation prior to the appointment.[31] Eventually, however, Slipyj, for "the good of the church" accepted the fait accompli and agreed to co-consecrate, together with the Pope, the new Archbishop-Metropolitan.[32]

One of the first public functions of the newly designated Archbishop was to be the official host to Pope John Paul II during the Pope's visit to the

Ukrainian Cathedral of the Immaculate Conception while on his first historic visit to the United States in October, 1979. Because of the turmoil among the Ukrainian Catholics over the patriarchal question, the Pope's visit to the Ukrainian Cathedral in Philadelphia had special significance. Members of the Ukrainian community began gathering at dawn on October 4 for a glimpse of the Pontiff, who arrived at the cathedral about 8:15 in the morning and remained in the resplendent interior, jammed with about 3000 exuberant people,[33] for about three-quarters of an hour. "It is a great honor for us to have him visit" a young woman replied to a reporter's query. "It shows he is aware of us and our special needs."[34]

Accompanied by Cardinals Augustine Casaroli, papal secretary of state, and Cardinal John Krol of Philadelphia, and other dignitaries, Pope John Paul was escorted down the red-carpeted main aisle of the cathedral as the voices of the combined church choir resounded in song. At the same time the exuberant throng greeted the Pope with spontaneous applause. Standing near the papal throne, placed in front of the royal doors of the Ikonostasis before the main altar, the Pope was formally greeted by Monsignor Lubachivsky, the metropolitan designate for the Ukrainian Catholics in America.

The Pope spoke briefly in Ukrainian and in English to the enthusiastic throng, many of whom had tears of joy and pride rolling down their faces. The Pontiff's leave-taking was equally moving. He bade farewell to each individual bishop and dignitary on the dais, gave a fatherly embrace to Msgr. Robert Moskal, in charge of the papal welcoming arrangements at the cathedral, and mixed with the school children, before leaving the church, again to the resonant voices of the choir and the applause and outcries of the throng. The genuine exuberance exhibited by the Ukrainians over the Pope's visit to their cathedral, will undoubtedly make that joyous event a high-point in the history of the Ukrainian Catholic Church in America.

On November 12, five weeks after his visit to the Ukrainian Cathedral in Philadelphia, together with Cardinal Slipyj and Metropolitan Hermaniuk, Pope John Paul II consecrated Lubachivsky as the Metropolitan for the Ukrainian Americans in the Vatican's Sistine Chapel. Five Ukrainian bishops assisted the Pope and

his co-consecrators in celebrating the Pontifical
Liturgy of consecration, witnessed by ten cardinals,
sixteen Latin rite bishops, along with many Ukrainian
clerics, sisters, seminarians, and hundreds of lay
persons.[35]

Archbishop Lubachivsky, the fourth Metropolitan
for the Ukrainian Catholics in America, was formally
installed in the Immaculate Conception Cathedral in
Philadelphia by the Apostolic Delegate, on December 4,
1979. Concelebrating the Liturgy with Lubachivsky
were Archbishops Hermaniuk and Kocisko and fourteen
Ukrainian and Transcarpathian bishops. Attending the
ceremonies were numerous Latin rite bishops, several
hundred priests and sisters, various officials, and
perhaps two thousand of the laity.[36]

The new Archbishop for Americans of Ukrainian
descent was born in Dolyna (Galicia), Western Ukraine
on June 24, 1914, the son of Eustachius and Anna
(Olijnyk) Lubachivsky. He entered the Theological
Academy in Lviv in 1934. After three years, Metropolitan Andrew Sheptytsky of Galicia sent him to
Innsbruck, Austria to continue his theological studies. He returned to Lviv where he was ordained by the
Metropolitan on September 21, 1938. After ordination
he returned to Innsbruck, then went to Sion,
Switzerland, during World War II, where he obtained
his Doctorate in Theology in 1941. During 1941-42 he
continued his studies in philosophy at the Pontifical
Gregorian University. In 1942 he began his studies at
the Pontifical Bible Institute in Rome, where he
earned a Master's Degree in Bible Studies in 1944. In
1945 he returned to his philosophical studies at
Gregorian University earning a Master's Degree in
Philosophy. During 1945-47 he studied medicine at
Rome's Royal Italian University.

Father Lubachivsky arrived in the United States
on May 29, 1947 and was assigned the duties of
secretary of the Ukrainian Catholic Committee for
Refugees and also appointed a teacher of German
and Ukrainian at St. Basil's Seminary in Stamford,
Connecticut. Late in 1948 he began a series of
brief assignments as assistant in parishes at
Hamtramck and North Branch, Michigan; Latrobe and
Wilkes-Barre, Pennsylvania; and Milwaukee, Wisconsin.
In 1951 he was assigned to Sts. Peter and Paul's
Ukrainian Church in Cleveland, Ohio. While in
Cleveland he bagan his scholarly writing, publishing

works in the fields of scripture, homiletics, and liturgics.

In 1968 Father Lubachivsky was named Spiritual Director of St. Josaphat's Seminary in Washington, D. C., from where he also served parishes in Monassas and Richmond, Virginia. In 1971 he began teaching at St. Basil's Academy for girls in Fox Chase, Pennsylvania, and in 1973 he became administrator of the Sacred Heart mission station associated with the Academy. In 1977 he was appointed Spiritual Director of St. Basil's Seminary in Stamford, a post he held when named Archbishop. In April of 1978 Pope Paul VI elevated him to the rank of Honorary Prelate.[37]

The controversy over Lubachivsky's appointment as the Metropolitan for the Ukrainian Americans was another indication that the turmoil among the Ukrainian Catholics, exacerbated by the patriarchal issue, had not been resolved. The question of the rights of the Ukrainian Church was the crux of the problem. Metropolitan Hermaniuk of Winnepeg, addressed the issue succinctly in his statement in 1979 on "The Unity of the Ukrainian Catholic Hierarchy".[38] According to Archbishop Hermaniuk, the Eastern Churches were demanding recognition of their canonical jurisdiction over all of their faithful, including those domiciled outside the territory of the Patriarchate or Major Archbishopric.

> For us Ukrainians, especially under the present circumstances, this is a matter of life and death for our Holy Ukrainian Catholic Church. Because, by not having the possibility of organizing our own religious life on our own territory, that is in the Ukraine, and by not having such a possibility beyond the Ukraine as well, our church is sentenced to a slow death. And that would be a tragedy not only for our Ukrainian people, but for the entire Universal Church.

In order to prevent such a tragedy the Ukrainians must, in the opinion of Archbishop Hermaniuk, insist that there is but one Ukrainian Catholic Church regardless of the territory in which its faithful reside or its bishops preside; and that she has one head, whether he is a Major Archbishop or a Patriarch, who leads under the authority of the successor of St.

Peter, the bishop of Rome. In a private audience with Pope John Paul on December 17, 1978, Metropolitan Hermaniuk learned that the Pontiff intended to assure the Ukrainian Church in the Ukraine, and beyond its territory, a single leadership. Therefore, the Ukrainian hierarchy, clergy, and laity, in the opinion of Hermaniuk, must coordinate their efforts to stop the disruptive process within their church; at the same time the hierarchy must continue to meet regularly while they await the recognition of the autonomy of the Ukrainian Church in exile.

4. Self-Government Achieved

Under the leadership of Cardinal Slipyj, the Ukrainian Catholic bishops continued to hold annual synods (considered as "conferences" of bishops by the Vatican). One such meeting was held on November 17-20, 1979, during which the participants expressed disapproval over the lack of consultation in the recent appointment of Monsignor Lubachivsky as Metropolitan of Philadelphia, and once again claimed recognition of a patriarchal structure for the Ukrainian Church, under which all episcopal appointments would be made by the Vatican in consultation with the Ukrainian bishops and with the approval of their primate, as is customary in other Eastern Churches in communion with Rome.

At the conclusion of their conference, on November 20, the bishops met with Pope John Paul. On February 5, 1980 the Pope informed Cardinal Slipyj, by letter, of his decision to convoke a synod of all Ukrainian bishops.[39] Two days later Cardinal Slipyj had a private audience with the Pope. Finally, on March 18, the Vatican made a public announcement that the Pontiff had called an extraordinary synod of Ukrainian bishops for March 24, 1980[40] at which the bishops would select a possible successor to eighty-eight year old Cardinal Slipyj, exiled Major Archbishop of Lviv. The naming of Slipyj's successor would assure the continuation of the visible leadership of the Ukrainian Catholic Church.

The synod, held in the Vatican, was attended by fifteen Ukrainian bishops, headed by Cardinal Slipyj. Three bishops, including Bishop Jaroslav Gabro from Chicago,[41] did not attend because of illness. It was the first time in the history of the Ukrainian Church that a synod of the Ukrainian bishops was convoked and presided over by the successor of St. Peter, the bishop of Rome. At the synod's opening Liturgy in the Sistine Chapel, Pope John Paul's homily delivered in Ukrainian, "suggested that one theme of the synod would be healing divisions among Ukrainian Catholics over a patriarchate."[42]

To the Ukrainian Catholics, this synod of Ukrainian bishops, the first to be authorized by the Vatican since 1929, had great historical significance. In essence, it meant recognition by the Vatican of the existence of the Ukrainian Catholic Church in the Ukraine, its right of self-government, and jurisdictional unity with it of all the Ukrainian Catholic episcopates throughout the world.[43]

On the closing day of the synod, March 27, the Vatican announced that Pope John Paul named Archbishop Lubachivsky of Philadelphia, first on a list of candidates selected by the Ukrainian bishops, as the coadjutor to Cardinal Slipyj and eventual successor to the head of the Ukrainian Catholic Church.[44] "With the nomination of Monsignor Lubachivsky, the continuation of the Ukrainian Catholic Church is assured" announced the Vatican daily L'Osservatore Romano. Since Lubachivsky is considered to be less "nationalistic" than Slipyj, declared another source, his appointment would tend to heal the division among the Ukrainians.[45]

One day after the closing of the extraordinary synod, on March 28, the Ukrainian Catholic Church in America lost another hiearch when Bishop Jaroslav Gabro of Chicago, who had been seriously ill with cancer, died at the age of sixty. The final funeral rites were held on April 1, at the Ukrainian St. Nicholas Cathedral in Chicago. The Requiem Liturgy was concelebrated by the new coadjutor to Cardinal Slipyj, Archbishop Lubachivsky, Archbishops Hermaniuk and Kocisko, together with nine other Ukrainian and Transcarpathian bishops. Also participating were: Cardinal John Cody, Archbishop of Chicago, who presided; Archbishop Constantine Buggan from Chicago, who represented the Ukrainian Orthodox Church; nine Latin rite bishops; about one hundred Ukrainian priests from America and Canada; about twenty-five Ukrainian sisters; numerous priests from other rites; civil officials; and about 1800 of the faithful.[46] The bishop's body was interred at St. Nicholas Cathedral cemetery. Until the selection and appoint-

ment of a successor, Msgr. William M. Bilinsky, chancellor of the diocese, administered the vacant See.

Less than a week after Bishop Gabro's funeral the
Ukrainian chancery of Philadelphia reported that
Archbishop Lubachivsky, now the administrator of the
archeparchy, would leave for Rome in mid-April to
confer with Cardinal Slipyj, who was contemplating
calling a regular synod of Ukrainian bishops to choose
candidates to succeed Lubachivsky as Metropolitan of
Philadelphia and, presumably, candidates to succeed
the late Bishop Gabro.[47]

During the ensuing months, several conferences of
Ukrainian bishops and audiences with the Pope by their
Archbishops followed before an agenda for a regular
synod of the Ukrainian Church was readied by a preparatory commission of seven bishops. With the approval of Pope John Paul, Cardinal Slipyj convened
the synod in Rome on November 25, 1980. The synod
closed on December 2; however, which one of the candidates presented by the Ukrainian bishops was selected
by the Pope was not disclosed until late the following
month. The newly appointed Apostolic Delegate in
Washington, Archbishop Pio Laghi, announced on January
29, 1981, that at the proposal of the Ukrainian
bishop's synod, Pope John Paul named Msgr. Stephen
Sulyk, pastor of the Church of the Assumption in Perth
Amboy, New Jersey, as Ukrainian Archbishop of Philadelphia and Metropolitan of the Ukrainian Catholics
in the United States. At the same time the Delegate
announced that Basilian Father Superior, Innocent
Lotocky, OSBM, pastor of the Immaculate Conception
Church in Hamtramck, Michigan, was named bishop of
the Ukrainian St. Nicholas Diocese in Chicago.

Msgr. Stephen Sulyk and the Very Rev. Innocent
Lotocky were consecrated bishops on March 1, 1981 by
Cardinal Slipyj the primate of the Ukrainian Catholic
Church. The colorful ceremony took place in the
Cardinal's Cathedral of St. Sophia on the outskirts of
Rome, with bishops Basil Losten of Stamford and Neil
Savaryn of Edmonton, Canada as co-consecrators. Pre-
sent at the colorful ceremonies were Cardinal
Wladyslaw Rubin, Prefect of the Sacred Congregation
for the Oriental Churches; Archbishop Mario Bruni, the
Secretary of the Congregation; and Archbishop Jean
Jadot, former Apostolic Delegate in the United States;
three additional Ukrainian bishops; thirty-six priests
(twenty from America); and about 300 faithful from

Europe and the United States.[48]

Archbishop Sulyk was formally installed at the Immaculate Conception Cathedral in Philadelphia in the afternoon of March 31, 1981 by the Apostolic Delegate, Archbishop Laghi. The ceremony of installation and Divine Liturgy was presided over by Archbishop Lubachivsky, in the presence of Cardinal Krol of Philadelphia, thirty-three archbishops and bishops of the Latin and Eastern rites, including Melkite rite Archbishop Joseph Tawil from West Norton, Mass., Bishop Francis M. Zayek from Detroit, Mich. of the Maronite rite, and Archbishop Constantine of Chicago representing the Ukrainian Orthodox Church in America. In addition to the distinguished members of the hierarchy, about 250 priests, 85 sisters, and about 2,500 of the faithful witnessed the impressive three-hour installation and Liturgy.[49]

The new Metropolitan for the American Ukrainian Catholics was born on October 2, 1924 in Balnycia, a Carpathian Mountain village in Lisco County in the western Ukrainian territory presently under Polish control, the son of Michael and Mary (Denys) Sulyk. He received his secondary education in the town of Sambir before the events of World War II forced him to flee his native land in 1944. After the war came to a close he entered the Ukrainian Seminary of the Holy Spirit, which was recently organized in Hirschberg, Germany. He emigrated to the United States in 1948 and continued his studies for the priesthood at St. Josephat's Seminary and the Catholic University in Washington, D. C., where he obtained his Licentiate Degree in Sacred Theology in 1952. He was ordained to the priesthood by the late Archbishop Constantine Bohachevsky at the Immaculate Conception Cathedral in Philadelphia on June 14, 1952. His first assignment was to assist in the organization of a new parish in Omaha, Nebraska, followed by assignments as assistant pastor at the Holy Spirit parish in Brooklyn, N. Y.; St. Nicholas, Minersville, Pa.; and Holy Trinity, Youngstown, Ohio. He became pastor of SS. Peter and Paul's Church in Phoenixville, Pa. in 1955, as well as secretary at the chancery office in Philadelphia. In 1957 he was assigned as pastor of St. Michael's parish in Frackville, Pa., and in 1961 he was transferred to St. Nicholas Church in Philadelphia. In 1962 he went to the Assumption Church in Perth Amboy, N. J., where he remained until named archbishop. In addition to his parish duties Father Sulyk had served as a

Diocesan Consultor, was a member of the Diocesan
Tribunal, Diocesan Administrative Board, and Vice-
Chairman of the Priest's Senate. In 1968, Pope Paul
VI raised him to the dignity of Papal Chaplain with
the title of Monsignor.[50]

On April 2, two days after his own installation
as the Metropolitan of the Ukrainian Catholics in
America, Archbishop Sulyk formally installed Bishop
Lotocky as the second bishop of St. Nicholas Diocese
of Chicago. With Archbishop Lubachivsky presiding,[51]
and in the presence of Cardinal John Cody of Chicago,
nearly two-thousand people filled the Cathedral of St.
Nicholas for the installation and Divine Liturgy.
Among those present were twenty-six Eastern and Western rite archbishops and bishops, Archbishop
Constantine representing the Ukrainian Orthodox
Church, over 150 priests, scores of sisters and monks,
and various governmental and civic officials.[52]

The new bishop of St. Nicholas Diocese of Chicago
was born on November 3, 1915 in Balkach, Western
Ukraine, the son of Stephen and Maria (Tytyn) Lotocky.
He entered the novitiate of the Basilian Fathers in
Krechiv in 1932. After completing his theological
studies in Dobromyl and Lavriv in the Ukraine, he was
ordained a priest by Bishop Paul Goydych on November
24, 1940 in Czechoslovakia. After ordination he
continued his theological studies and in 1945 he was
awarded a Doctorate in Sacred Theology at Vienna,
Austria. Prior to his emigration to America he
served the Ukrainian immigrant community in Belgium.
Father Lotocky arrived in the United States in 1946
taking up residence at the Basilian Father's monastery
in Dawson, Pa. (near Pittsburgh), where, for a time,
he was Acting Provincial of the American province of
the order. In 1957 he was named pastor of St.
George's Ukrainian Church in New York City where he
also became the superior of the Basilian Fathers assigned to that church. In 1958 he was transferred to
the Basilian Novitiate in Glen Cove, L. I., New York,
where he became Director of Novices. In 1961 he was
named pastor of St. Nicholas Church in Chicago,
Illinois, and superior of the Basilian Fathers at that
location. After St. Nicholas became the cathedral
church for the newly created Ukrainian Diocese of
Chicago in 1961, he was transferred to the Immaculate
Conception Church in Hamtramck, Michigan, where he was
pastor and superior of the Basilian Fathers there
until appointed to succeed the late Bishop Gabro.[52]

After experiencing rather unexpected losses and changes within its leadership in the last few years, the American Ukrainian Catholic Church in mid-1981 appears to have regained that stability of leadership which it seemed to lack in much of the 1970's. Pope John Paul II's decision to recognize, in part, the Ukrainian Catholic Church's right of self-government, (a goal that its Major Archbishop, Cardinal Slipyj revived at the Vatican Council) has begun to heal the divisions among the Ukrainian Catholics in America over the patriarchate. In addition, the Pope's choice of European-born nominees as ordinaries (each, however, with more than thirty years of pastoral experience in America) may also begin to dissipate the divisions between the old and the post-World-War-II Ukrainian immigrations.[53]

It is to be hoped that, in the 1980's, the decade in which Ukrainian churches throughout the world will be commemorating the millenium of Christianity in the Ukraine, the Ukrainian Catholics in America can turn their main energies from the divisive problems they faced in the 1970's towards solving the most pressing one, expressed in the words of the new Metropolitan in his first public address following his consecration in Rome: "the most serious problem and the one which is cardinal to the cure of all other ills, is the shortage of priestly and religious vocations.... We must bend our energies to explore, discover, and adapt new and effective solutions to this problem. ..."[54]

CONCLUDING REMARKS

The American Ukrainian Catholics, who will celebrate the centenary of their church in 1984, have indeed made great strides since 1884. Whereas in the
latter part of the nineteenth century few Latin rite
American Catholics had any knowledge of Eastern rite
Catholics, today there are few indeed who are still
unfamiliar with their Eastern Catholic neighbors. In
the early years of the current century very few Latin
bishops or clergy were ready to accept a separate and
independent Byzantine rite episcopate in the United
States, but today few bishops seem to question the
existence of five independent Eastern rite jurisdictions in this country.[1] Even as late as the mid-
1930's serious doubt existed concerning the future of
the Byzantine Catholic Church in America. The creation by the Holy See, however, of the independent
ecclesiastical province of Philadelphia for the Ukrainian Catholics in 1958, the first Byzantine rite
ecclesiastical province in the United States, helped
to dissipate such fears. Prior to 1958 this Church
was still technically considered a missionary church,
dependent on European sources for its actual existence; in the late 1950's it became the source of
newly-ordained bishops for Ukrainian immigrants in
such western European countries as England and
Germany.

The American Ukrainian Catholic Church in the
United States has matured and taken on permanent
characteristics, but, as with any living organism,
its development will have to continue. (See appendix
3). Further progress will have to be made, particularly in that intangible area of unqualified acceptance by the overwhelmingly more numerous and influential Latin rite. The much-to-be-hoped-for total
acceptance has been brought closer to fruition by the
Second Vatican Council and its Decree on Eastern
Catholic Churches, which fixes the relations between
the Latin and the Oriental Churches; however, the
implementation of the expressed wishes of the Ecumenical Council remains to be fully realized. That
it is not fully realized is reflected in the words

of the Jesuit scholar, Rev. Robert Clement: "Today
the Catholic Church lives according to one tradition
only, the Latin tradition. Historically, though,
there were two..."[2] The complexity of the situation
is voiced, finally, by Msgr. Basil Shereghy, a scholar
of the Eastern tradition:

> As the idea of America as a melting
> pot is incorrect and injurious, so also
> the idea of uniformity in the Catholic
> Church is erroneous. In the one, holy,
> catholic and apostolic Church there are
> Christians of different traditions, dif-
> ferent theological interpretations, dif-
> ferent spiritual practices and different
> liturgical rites. All Catholics, regard-
> less of their rites, geographical loca-
> tion and spiritual heritage, are 'of
> equal dignity, so that none of them is
> superior to the others' (Vat. II, Decree
> on the Eastern Catholic Churches, No. 3).
> By learning about each other, we will all
> grow in knowledge, in faith, in love.[3]

APPENDIX 1 *

Ruthenian priests, their European origin, and the location of their American parishes in 1896.

Galician origin:

1. Theophan Obushkevich, Olyphant and Mayfield, Pa.
2. John Konstankevich, Shamokin, Pa.
3. Nestor Dmytriv, Mt. Carmel, Pa.
4. Michael Stefanovich, Pittsburgh, Pa.
5. John Ardan, Jersey City, N. J.

Transcarpathian origin, Munkacs diocese:

6. Nicephor Khanat, Scranton, Pa.
7. Eugene Volkay, New York City
8. Alexander Dzubay, New Haven, Conn.
9. Theodore Damjanovich, Trenton, N. J.
10. Cornelius Lavrisin, Shenandoah, Pa.
11. Augustine Lavrisin, Mahonoy City, Pa.
12. Eugene Satala, Passaic, N. J.
13. John Hrabar, Philadelphia, Pa.
14. Basil Voloshyn, Yonkers, N. Y.
15. G. Dzubay, Johnstown, Pa.
16. Stephen Jackovich, Duquesne, Pa.
17. John Sabov, Lindsey, Pa.
18. Acacius Kaminski, Hazleton, Pa.: Pine Street
19. Victor Balogh, Trauger, Pa.
20. Nicholas Stecovic, Braddock, Pa.
21. Nicholas Sherehely, Streator, Ill.
22. Nicholas Ilashevich, Wilkes-Barre, Pa.
23. Dr. S. Sabov, Cleveland, Ohio
24. Ireneus Matyackov, Ramey, Pa.

Transcarpathian origin, Presov diocese:

25. Cyril Gulovich, Freeland, Pa.
26. Vladimir Molchanyi, Kingston, Pa.
27. Nicholas Molchanyi, McAdoo, Pa.
28. V. Martyak, Hazleton, Pa.
29. Gabriel Martyak, Lansford, Pa.

Note: Rev. Gregory Hrushka, previously pastor in Jersey City, and Rev. I. Zaklynsky from Old Forge, Pa. seceded to the Russian Orthodox Church.

---

* Pershy kalendar, 1897, pp. 168-169.

APPENDIX 2 *

Number of Ruthenian Churches by States in 1904:

Pennsylvania	57
Ohio	10
New York	9
New Jersey	6
Connecticut	4
West Virginia	3
Indiana	2
Illinois	2
Massachusetts	1
Missouri	1
Total	95

Origin and number of Ruthenian priests in America in 1904:

Hungary:	
Munkacs	32
Presov	14
Galicia:	
Lviv	8
Peremishl	6
Stanislaviv	3
United States:	
Scranton	2
Hungary:	
Basilian Father (OSBM)	1
Galicia:	
Basilian Father (OSBM)	1
Total	67

---

*Kalendar Sojedinenija, 1905, p. 160.

APPENDIX 3 *

General Statistics of the Ukrainian Catholic Church
in America in 1981

	Phila. Arch-Eparchy	Stamford Eparchy	Chicago Eparchy
Archbishops	1	-	-
Bishops	1**	1	1**
Priests	136	78	45
Diocesan	96	53	26
Religious	12	19	13
Active outside Diocese	2	1	4
Retired, ill, etc.	26	5	3
Permanent Deacons	2	-	2
Brothers	1	20	-
Sisters	210	49	20
Parishes	111	52	36
With Resident Pastor	96	40	25
Non-resident Pastor	15	12	11
Missions	15	9	4
Chapels	32	9	4
With Resident Chaplain	6	2	-
Non-resident Chaplain	26	7	4
Seminaries	1	1	-
Seminarians	33	13	4
Colleges	1	1	-
Students	304	12	-
High Schools	1	1	1
Students	341	114	133
Elementary Schools, Parochial	15	9	3
Students	2,373	956	840
Total Youths under Catholic Instruction (including Public School pupils in Special Religious Instruction Classes)	6,333	2,393	2,083
Teachers	206	108	59
Priests (full time)	6	12	2
Sisters	58	23	20
Lay Teachers	142	73	37
Homes for invalid and aged	3	1	-
Guests	406	20	-

	Phila. Arch-Eparchy	Stamford Eparchy	Chicago Eparchy
Baptisms	782	358	419
Infant	747	346	362
Converts	35	12	57
Marriages	471	202	231
Catholic	343	165	189
Mixed	128	37	42
Deaths	799	477	321
Total Catholic Population	167,419	47,094	30,128

---

*CD, 1981, pp. 690; 812; 927.

**Appointed bishop after the publication of the 1981 Directory.

BIBLIOGRAPHY AND FOOTNOTES

The bibliography is in the footnotes. The writer read numerous sources not mentioned in the footnotes, but since they were not quoted they are not included.

INTRODUCTION

1. Several interpretations are advanced concerning the coming of Christianity to the territory of Kiev. The relatively recent work by K. Ericson, "The Earliest Conversion of the Rus' to Christianity", Slavonic and East European Review, XLIV (January, 1966), 98-121, suggests that Kiev was converted for the first time to Christianity early in the ninth century during the time of Ky, the founder of Kiev, and that Ky was the first Christian ruler of the territory and not Askold and Dyr. Similarly, different views are held by scholars concerning the details of Vladimir's baptism and of the organization of the Kievan Church. For a comparatively recent discussion by a Ukrainian scholar see Nicholas Chubaty, Istoria Christiianstva na Rusy-Ukraini (Rome, 1965).

2. The Byzantine rite is the name applied to the forms and laws developed by the Church of Constantinople (Byzantium) and later adopted by other areas influenced by its civilization. In time particular rules and regulations developed among the different peoples, consequently, different disciplines within the Byzantine rite emerged. The discipline followed by the Ukrainians, and other Slavic groups, used Church-Slavonic as their language of worship prior to the reforms of Vatican II -- thus the term, Byzantine-Slavic rite.

3. Oscar Halecki, Borderlands of Western Civilization (New York, 1952), p. 34.

4. Victor J. Pospishil, Interritual Canon Law Problems in the United States and Canada (Chesapeake City, Md., 1955), p. 15. For a useful discussion of the terminology used in papal documents to distinguish between the Ruthenians

and the Muscovites see the introductory remarks
of P. Athanasius G. Welykyj (ed.), <u>Documenta
Pontificum Romanorum Historiam Ucrainae
Illustrantia</u> (Rome, 1953), I, xiii-xvi.

5. Most of the American descendants of the
Ruthenian immigrants from Transcarpathia in
Hungary (the southern slopes of the Carpathian
mountains) accept the name <u>Rusyn</u>. Although the
ancestors of the Transcarpathian Rusyns were
anthropologically and linguistically related to
the ancestors of the Ukrainians, cultural and
political differences have developed between
their descendants because of the dissimilar socio-
economic and political fortunes of the Rusyns
under Hungarian control and of the Ukrainians
under Austrian rule. Since the Second World War,
the territory of Transcarpathia (with the exception of the extreme western part which politically belongs to Czechoslovakia) has been a part
of the Ukrainian Soviet Republic.

6. The faithful of the Ruthenian discipline of the
Byzantine rite are often referred to as "Greek
Catholics." The term has proven to be mislead-
ing. (Father Gregory Hrushka recommended that it
be dropped from use as early as 1893. See
"Poznaimo sia", <u>Svoboda</u> (Jersey City, N. J.),
October 15, 1893, p. 1. It is often associated
either with the Greek Orthodox or with the Greek
nationality, while the Ruthenians are in communion with the church of Rome and they are neither
of the Greek nationality nor do they use Greek as
the liturgical language. Ecclesiastically speaking, the term Ruthenian has been extended to include also such Byzantine rite people as the
Hungarians and the Croats. On the other hand, in
recent years the Papacy has begun to use the term
"Ukrainian rite" when referring to the Ukrainian
Catholics. A still useful general discussion of
the problem of ecclesiastical terminology is to
be found in Clement C. Englert's "Consistent
Oriental Terminology," <u>Homiletic and Pastoral
Review</u>, XXXXIII, (September, 1943), 1077-1082.

7. The national consciousness of many of the
Ruthenians did not fully develop until the current century, consequently the term Ruthenian
also found its place in the American immigration
records, thus adding to the confusion about the
national origin of the immigrants so listed.
Today, the national name Ukrainian is used by the
descendants of the immigrants from Galicia and

Bukovina, while the names Rusyn or Ruthenian are preferred by those originating from Trans-carpathia. For a brief discussion concerning the historical evolution in the use of the terms Rus and Ukraine, see below, pp. 8-9.

CHAPTER I

1. Julian Chupka, "Obrazky z Ameryky," Svoboda, March 19, 1896, pp. 1-2 (cont. on pp. 1-2 of the next two issues) provides interesting first-hand illustrations.
2. About one third of the early Slovak immigrants were of the Byzantine-Slavic rite according to P. V. Rovnianek, "The Slovaks in America," Charities, XIII (December 3, 1904), 240. They were most likely Slovakized Transcarpathians. Rovnianek was editor of a Slovak daily and an organizer of the National Slovak Society.
3. The effects of the new immigrant labor on the anthracite region of Pennsylvania is discussed in detail by Frank J. Warne, The Slav Invasion of the Mine Workers, (Philadelphia, 1904). Unfortu-nately, however, Warne applies the term Slav to all non-English speaking immigrants from Southern and Eastern Europe, consequently, the work con-tributes only limited information regarding the Ruthenians, almost all of whom in the beginning worked in and about the coal mines. Far from weakening labor organization, the Ruthenians, along with other Slavic groups in the anthracite region, became an essential element in the estab-lishment of unionism in the coal industry by the early 1900s. For an exposition of this thesis, see Victor Greene, The Slavic Community on Strike (Notre Dame, 1968).
4. M. J. Hanchin, "Istoria Sojedinenija iz pervych lit," Kalendar Greko Kaftoliceskaho Sojedinenija, 1937, (Homestead, Pa.), p. 42. Hanchin came to America in the early 1900's and in 1914 became editor-in-chief of the influencial Amerikansky Russky Viestnik (Munhall, Pa.), hereafter cited as the Viestnik. A valuable reference work on the Ruthenians in America appeared with the pub-lication, late in 1979, of a Guide to the Amerikansky Russky Viestnik. Volume I: 1894-1914, compiled by James M. Evans. Entry number 4002 on page 249 lists the following title rele-vant to early Ruthenian immigration: "Vyselenie

Halycyskych y Uhorskych Rusynov v Ameryku y ych
sorhanizovanie," January 9, 1894, p. 2. The
present writer, unfortunately, was unable to make
use of that article prior to the publication of
this work.

5. Nestor Dmytriw, "Pershi roky emigratsii ukrai-
ntsiv v Zluchenykh Derzhavakh Piv. Ameryky,"
Kalendar Provydinia, 1924, (Philadelphia), pp.
161-162. A useful statistical skeleton of the
source and distribution of the new Ruthenian immigration (also its political, economic and educational characteristics), based on the report of
the Commissioner of Immigration, is provided by
Kate Holloday Claghorn, in "Slavs, Magyars, and
Some Others in the New Immigration," Charities,
XIII, 199-205.

6. Dmytriw, "Pershi roky," pp. 161-162.

7. Julian Bachynsky, Ukrainska imigratsia v
Ziedynenykh Derzhavakh Ameryky, (Lviv, 1914), p.
88. This is an extremely useful secondary source
for the early history of the Ukrainians in America.

8. Immigration reports indicate that in the twelve
fiscal years from 1899 to 1910 inclusive, 98.2
per cent of the Ruthenians admitted to the United
States came from Austria-Hungary. See U. S.
Senate, Dictionary of Races or Peoples, Reports
of the Immigration Commission, Doc. No. 662, 61st
Cong. 3d Sess., 1911, IX, 118. Hereafter cited
as Dictionary of Races.

9. Andrew J. Shipman, "Our Russian Catholics; the
Greek Ruthenian Church in America," The Messenger
(New York), XLII (November, 1904), 575-576.

10. For a discussion of economic and other causes of
emigration by a very active Ukrainian pioneer see
John Ardan, "The Ruthenians in America,"
Charities, XIII. 246-252. The U. S. immigration
reports contain statistical information concerning the causes of emigration from Austria-Hungary
and the characteristics of that immigration to
the United States. See U. S. Senate, Emigration
Conditions in Europe, Doc. No. 748, 61st Cong.,
3d Sess., 1911, XII, 361-384.

11. The first educated immigrant of whom there is
available record was a political exile from the
Russian empire, Agapius Honcharenko, a Ukrainian
Orthodox priest, who arrived in 1865. After
teaching Greek in an Episcopal school, transla-
ting for the American Bible Society, and working
for newspapers in New York, Honcharenko moved to

San Francisco in 1867 and was not seriously involved with the mass immigration which began in
the late 1870's. Incidentally, upon his arrival
on the west coast, Honcharenko found that there
were other Ukrainian political exiles living in
California. He organized them into a "Decembrist
club," which was probably the first such Slavic
political organization in America. See Wasyl
Halich, Ukrainians in the United States (Chicago,
1937), p. 21. Reprinted New York, 1970.

12. Warne, The Slav Invasion, pp. 113-116, comments
on the most common exploiters of the Slavs. The
social, economic and educational problems faced
by the immigrants are also profitably discussed
by Peter Roberts, "The Sclavs in Anthracite Coal
Communities," Charities, XIII pp. 215-222, and by
Mary Buell Sayles, "Housing and Social Conditions
in a Slavic Neighborhood," Ibid., pp. 257-261.
The above authors, incidentally, are examples of
early American writers deeply interested in the
problems of the new immigrants from Eastern
Europe. The December 3, 1904 issue of Charities
represents an early attempt by an American jour-
nal (non-ecclesiastic) to provide a comprehensive
and authoritative coverage of the new immigrants.

13. K., "Istoriia pershoi ruskoi tserkvy v Shenandoah,
Pa.," Pershy rusko-amerykansky kalendar, ed.
Nestor Dmytrov (Mount Carmel, Pa., 1897), p. 134.
Hereafter cited as Persky kalendar.

14. The immigrants' letter cited in Svoboda, October
10, 1894, p. 1, (article entitled "Pro rusku
emigratsiiu").

15. Letter of Metropolitan Sembratovich cited by
Isidore Sochockyj, "Ukrainska Katolytska Tserkva
vizantyisko-slovianskoho obriadu v ZDA",
Ukrainska Katolytska Mytropolia v Zluchenykh
Derzhavakh Ameryky, (Philadelphia, 1959), pp.
200-201.

16. K., "Istoriia pershoi tserkvy," in Pershy
kalendar, p. 134, lists the following individuals
as working most diligently to raise money for
Father Volansky's passage to America: George
Huretiak, Paul Matiash, Andrew Kosar, Stephen
Shvetz, Michael Kushvara, Simeon Kotsur, Andrew
Bishko, S. Krajniak, Simeon Kuryla, Wasyl Mizhik,
Alex Fedorchak. Collectors visited the Penn-
sylvania communities of Shenandoah, Shamokin,
Excelsior, and Hazleton.

17. John Volansky, "Spomyny z davnykh lit:, Svoboda,
September 5, 1912, p. 4. Other very useful early

123

sources, although sometimes conflicting in detail, on the problems and accomplishments of Father Volansky are: "A Noted Character, An American Priesthood of one and What He Has Accomplished", Evening Herald, (Shenandoah), May 30, 1887, p. 4; Michael Pavlyk, "Pochatky ukrainskoi organizatsii na chuzhyni" (excerpts of Pavlyk's article published in 1888) Kalendar Ukrainskoho Narodnoho Soyuza, 1920 (Jersey City, 1919), pp. 52-54; Hraf Lelyva, "Polozhenie rusynov v Spoluchenikh Derzhavakh Povnochnoy Ameryky", Pershy kalendar, p. 47-67. Wherever conflicts occurred the writer relied on the statements of Father Volansky.

18. Volansky, "Spomyny," p. 4. According to the Byzantine-Slavic rite traditions married as well as single men were ordained to the priesthood.

19. H. J. Heuser, "Greek Catholics and Latin Priests", American Ecclesiastical Review, IV (March, 1891), 195-196. Hereafter cited as AER. Father Heuser, professor at St. Charles Seminary at Overbrook, Pennsylvania, and editor of the AER, was one of the first Latin rite priests to acquaint himself thoroughly with and write about the Ruthenian Catholics in America.

20. For the first month or two Father Volansky also rented two small rooms in this hall until more suitable living quarters were located in a house on Coal Street.

21. The first child baptized in the chapel was Maria Marusyn, daughter of Michael and Anna Marusyn on December 25, 1884; the first marriage took place on January 9, 1885, between Michael Pringel and Maria Ivanko, children of John and Maria Pringel and Simeon and Dorothy Ivanko, from Saros, Hungary; the first funeral service was held for Maria Fedorczak, a child of Alexander and Maria Fedorczak from Ripky Sanok, Galicia, on January 25, 1885. See St. Michael's Diamond Jubilee Book, (Shenandoah, 1959), p. 9 (unnumbered). Hereafter cited as St. Michael's Book.

22. Victor R. Greene, The Slavic Community on Strike (Notre Dame, 1968), pp. 87, 106.

23. Volansky, "Spomyny," p. 4.

24. Evening Herald, May 30, 1887, p. 4.

25. The first Byzantine-Slavic rite Mass in New York City was celebrated in the basement of St. Brigid's Church on Avenue A, on April 19, 1890, but there was no Ruthenian church in Manhattan until the opening of St. George's Church in 1895.

See Andrew J. Shipman, "Greek Catholics in
America," Catholic Encyclopedia, VI, (1909), 748.
Hereafter cited as CE. Shipman was one of the
first American authors to become intimately acquainted with the problems of the Slavic immigrants. His activities in behalf of the
Ruthenian immigrants and their church should not
be overlooked. In 1895, for instance, he helped
to organize St. George's Church on East 20th
Street. The Parish later moved to East 7th
Street, between Second and Third Avenues, where
the property was bought for $90,000 with the
entire transaction handled by Shipman as counsel
for the church. Partially for the dedication of
the new church on East 7th Street, Shipman prepared and later published a translation of The
Holy Mass According to the Greek Rite (New York,
1912). This pamphlet of forty-four pages containing double columns, the Slavic version and
Shipman's English version, was the first English
translation of the Byzantine-Slavic Liturgy of
St. John Chrysostom ever made. The high esteem
with which Shipman was held by the Ukrainian-
Americans is illustrated by the following two
examples: a long biographical article on
Shipman in Svoboda, September 8, 1910, p. 4 gives
Shipman full credit for informing the American
public about the Ukrainians. Secondly, upon
Shipman's death in 1915, after a Requiem Mass in
New York's St. Patrick's Cathedral, a burial ser-
vice was conducted by Bishop Soter Ortynsky, the
first Ukrainian bishop in the United States.
This was the first time, incidentally, that a
Byzantine-Slavic rite burial service was seen in
a Latin rite church in the United States. See
Conde B. Pallen's interesting "Biographical
Sketch of Andrew J. Shipman" in A Memorial of
Andrew J. Shipman, ed. Conde B. Pallen, (New York,
1916), pp. elv-lxv. Hereafter cited as Shipman
Memorial.

26. Bachynsky, Ukrainska imigratsiia, p. 288.
27. At the time of his inquiry, in 1890, Rev. Heuser
reported that there were nine properly accredited priests in the United States:
1. Rev. Theophan Obushkevich (from Galicia) at
   Shamokin, Shenandoah, and Mahonoy City, Pa.
2. Rev. Alexis Tovt (Hungary) at Minneapolis,
   Minn.
3. Rev. John Zapototsky (Hungary) at Kensington,
   Pa.

4. Rev. Gregory Hrushka (Galicia) at Jersey City, N. J.
5. Rev. Alexander Dzubay (Hungary) at Hazleton, Pa.
6. Rev. Eugene Volkay (Hungary) at Hazleton, Pa.
7. Rev. Gabriel Vislotsky (Hungary) at Olyphant, Pa.
8. Rev. Cyril Gulovich (Hungary) at Freemont, Pa.
9. Rev. Stephen Jackovich (Hungary) at McKeesport, Pa.

   See AER, IV (March 1891), 197-198 (footnote).

28. Svoboda, November 21, 1894, p. 1.
29. Pershy kalendar, pp. 168-169. Except for the fact that several of the priests seceded to the Russian Orthodox Church the total number of priests would be greater.
30. The Ruthenian immigration figures are particularly inaccurate. Many of the immigrants from Austria-Hungary were listed as Austrians, Hungarians, Poles, Slovaks, Russians, etc. The Viestnik, indicates on page one of its March 6, 1894 issue that it was read in the United States by 250,000 Byzantine rite Catholics. Svoboda, October 10, 1894, indicates that the total immigration in America was about 200,000. Fourteen months later, however, (December 5, 1895) the same paper provides 300,000 as the estimate of the population at that time, which would appear to be too great an increase over the previous figure. Considering that the immigration statistics indicate a steady growth of immigration up to the First World War, and taking into consideration the immigration figures which indicate that during the twelve fiscal years 1899-1910 inclusive 147,375 Ruthenians were admitted to the United States (Dictionary of Races, p. 118), it would appear that the estimate of 200,000 immigrants in the mid 1890's, after twenty years of ever increasing immigration, is a responsible one. Obviously the estimated 500,000 Ruthenians in America as shown by a chart on page 118 of the Dictionary of Races, indicating the number and distribution of those immigrants in 1897, must be a typographical error.
31. Even business men who were not Catholics or Ruthenian would, for business purposes, become organizers of congregations and the leaders of their church building programs. See Svoboda, November 21, 1894, p. 1.
32. Bachynsky, Ukrainska imigratsia, p. 264.

33. Ibid., p. 386.
34. According to the figures in Kalendar Sojedinenija,
    1900, p. 204, there were fifty-five Ruthenian
    Catholic Churches in the United States in 1899
    which were served by thirty-nine priests. Twenty-
    one of the priests came from Munkacs (Mukachiv)
    and nine from Presov (Priashiv) in Transcarpathia,
    whereas there were only six from Peremishl and
    two from Yaroslav in Galicia. In addition there
    was also a Basilian Father from Transcarpathia.
35. Bachynsky, Ukrainska imigratsia, p. 290.
36. Several theories are advanced concerning the
    origin and meaning of the word Ukraine. See e.g.,
    R. Smal-Stocki, "Origin and meaning of the name
    Ukraine" (Svoboda, No. 66, 1950), M. Andrusiak,
    Nazva "Ukraina" (Chicago: 1951), and J. B.
    Rudnyckyj, The Term and Name "Ukraine",
    Onamastica I (Winnipeg, 1951). The name was
    popularized in the seventeenth century as a re-
    sult of the Polish-Cossack wars in the 1640's and
    1650's, and in particular, by Guilliame Le
    Vasseur de Beauplan's Description d'Ukraine
    (first published in 1650) and a number of his
    maps. For an account of de Beauplan's and other
    foreign descriptions of the Ukraine, see
    Volodymyr Sichynsky, Ukraine in Foreign Comments
    and Descriptions (New York, 1953).
37. For general information on the various names ap-
    plied to the territory of the Ukraine and its
    people in different periods, see, e.g., P.
    Kovaliv, "Name of Ukraine in Foreign Languages",
    The Ukrainian Quarterly VI (December, 1950),
    346-351; also, the articles by G. Shevelov, J. B.
    Rudnyckyj, O. Pritsak, and the general remarks by
    Z. Kuzela in Ukraine: A Concise Encyclopaedia
    (Toronto, 1963), I, 3-12.
38. Sochockyj, "Ukrainska Tserkva," p. 200. For a
    useful discussion of the Ruthenians in the
    Habsburg lands of Galicia, Transcarpathia, and
    Bukovina in the second half of the nineteenth
    century, see Robert A. Kann's The Multinational
    Empire (New York, 1955), I, 318-332. For a
    general discussion on the Ruthenians see Shipman's
    "Ruthenians", CE. XIII (1912), 278-280.
39. Shipman, "Greek Catholics," 749. See also his
    "Our Russian Catholics; the Greek Ruthenian
    Church in America," The Messenger, XLII (Decem-
    ber, 1904), 664, for a variation of this divi-
    sion beginning in 1895. The Moscophile, or
    Russophile, movement was supported by many

Russian leaders and it became an expedient means
of fostering Russian Panslavism and imperialism.

40. Stephen C. Gulovich, "The Rusin Exarchate in the
United States," Eastern Churches Quarterly, VI
(October-December, 1946), 463. Hereafter cited
as ECQ.

41. See Shipman, "Immigration to the United States",
Shipman Memorial, p. 92; Victor Greene, For God
and Country: The Rise of Polish and Lithuanian
Ethnic Consciousness in America, 1860-1900
(Madison, 1975), pp. 10-13; and below, pp.
11-14.

42. An illustration of the major role of the clergy
in the organization and administration of the
Sojedinenije is provided in the "Istorija Greko
Kaft. Sojedinenija", Kalendar Sojedinenija,
1942, pp. 39-74.

43. An excellent account of the role of the clergy in
the organization and administration of the Soyuz
is provided by Nestor Dmytriw (Dmytrov) "Korotkyj
nacerk istorijy rozvoju Ruskoho Narodnoho Sojuzu",
Kalendar Soyuza, 1914, pp. 36-101.

44. See the brief discussions concerning these matters by Shipman, "Our Russian Catholics," 664,
and by Bachynsky, Ukrainska imigratsia, 431-432.

45. The term "priest-radicals" was the common derog-
atory name applied to these priests and their
cohorts by the opposition. See, for example,
Viestnik, March 7, 14, 21, 1902.

46. Emily Balch, "A Shepherd of Immigrants,"
"Charities," XIII, pp. 193-194. Balch was one of
the early American scholars interested in the
problems of the new immigrants from Eastern
Europe.

47. Letter of Cardinal Miecislaus Ledochowski, Prefect of the Sacred Congregation of the Propagation of Faith, to Cardinal James Gibbons of
Baltimore, dated May 10, 1892, advising the
American bishops of the instructions addressed to
the Ruthenian bishops in Austro-Hungary in 1890,
AER, VII, 66-67. Earlier decrees were not made,
most likely, because this immigration was deemed
to be of temporary nature. According to Bachynsky,
Ukrainska imigratsia, p. 89, however, contrary to
general opinion, the early immigration was not of
a temporary nature but a permanent one. Almost
90 percent of these immigrants remained permanently in the United States. Bachynsky admits it
was true that originally these workers thought of
going back to the old country after working a

year or two. However, the fact remains that for the most part these intentions were changed while in America, and the vast majority of them never returned to their homeland. The change in character from a temporary to a permanent type of immigration was particularly evident from about the middle of the 1890's according to Ardan, "Ruthenians," 249.

48. Letter of Cardinal Ledochowski, AER, VII, 67.
49. The attitude of the American Latin rite bishops towards the Ruthenians, to paraphrase a 1893 source, seems to have been as follows: since it was difficult to induce the Ruthenians to Roman Catholic parishes, and in order that they not be lost to the faith, it was best to recognize the Ruthenian priests in America in the hope that by the next generation the Ruthenians would accept the customs of the Latin Church. See "United Greek Catholics", The Catholic Times (Philadelphia), February 25, 1893, p. 1. On occasion, the instructions from Rome blatantly favored the Latin rite over the Ruthenian. A ruling in 1897 reads, in part: "Children born in America of foreign parents whose native language is not English are not obliged when of age to become members of the parish to which their parents belong... Catholics not born in America, but knowing the English language, have the right of becoming members of a parish in which English is in use." See "An Important Decision," The Catholic Herald (New York), June 5, 1897, p. 8.
50. Heuser, "Greek Catholics," p. 198. Cardinal Ledochowski's letter, AER, VII, 67, also makes specific reference to the petitions by some of the priests for permission to remain in America, as well as to their seeking the establishment of an Apostolic Vicariate of their rite.
51. Bachynsky, Ukrainska imigratsia, p. 296.
52. According to Bachynsky, p. 296, the priests who originated from the Munkacs Diocese were pronounced sympathizers of the Hungarian cause. Generally speaking, they had succeeded in gaining most of the bigger and wealthier parishes. The priests from the Diocese of Presov were of less aristocratic background than those from Munkacs and represented the opposite Transcarpathian faction generally claiming a cultural communion with the Ukrainians from Austrian Galicia and Bukovina.
53. Svoboda, March 5, 1896, p. 1, also May 14, 1896,

p. 1, illustrates the strong tone of these appeals.

54. Ibid., June 6, 1901, p. 2, June 13, p. 2, and June 27, p. 2, provide additional information by the leading priests of the association.

55. Ibid., June 6, 1901, p. 2.

56. Ibid., February 21, 1901, p. 2.

57. Ibid., April 10, 1902, p. 2 and May 15, p. 4, contain an extended report of the Convention's radical discussions and resolutions.

58. The radical views of the association of the Ruthenian Church in America towards Rome, Metropolitan Sheptytsky of Galicia, and towards the American hierarchy are well illustrated in the association's booklet Uniia v Amerytsi (New York, 1902), which explains their position in reply to Metropolitan Sheptytsky's letter of August 20, 1902. The document is concluded with the signatures of the chairman of the association's general committee, and the chairman of the clerical committee. The Transcarpathian faction strongly opposed this association. See, for example, the Viestnik editorials, March 7, 14, and 21, 1902, p. 4.

59. Bishop Hoban's letter of excommunication, dated February 22, 1902, followed Ardan's strongly anti-Rome article entitled "Skazhim sobi pravdu v ochy", Svoboda, February 13, 1902, p. 2. Numerous reports on Ardan's excommunication and the court fight over the Olyphant Church are found in Svoboda, especially in the April to June issues of 1902. The Viestnik took the opposite view of these events from that of Svoboda. See, for instance, Viestnik editorial, March 28, 1902, p. 4.

60. According to Father Tovt's own story, cited in the Amerikanskii Pravoslavnyi Viestnik, II (July 13, 1898), 619, because of his difficulties with Archbishop John Ireland of St. Paul, he petitioned the Russian Orthodox bishop in San Francisco and was received by Bishop Vladimir into the Russian Orthodox Church on March 25, 1891. Tovt became an energetic advocate of the Russian Orthodox Church among the Ruthenians in America and a bitter opponent of Catholicism. (See "Vozsoedinenie z pravoslavnoiu tserkoviiu Minneapoliskago prikhoda", Kalendar Pravosl. obshch. Vzaimopomoshchi, 1901, cited by A. Levkov in "Tsareslaviie a Rusyni v Amerytse", Svoboda, April 11, 1901, p. 4.) It is said that he was the cause of nearly 10,000 Ruthenian Catholics seceding to the Orthodox Church. (See

Andrew J. Shipman, "Greek Orthodox Church in
America", CE, VI, [1909]. 772-773.) Tovt's ag-
gressive attempts to transfer Ruthenian Catholic
Churches to Russian Orthodox control is illus-
trated by the long struggle for the control of
the church in Wilkes-Barre, Pa. which started in
1893 and was not concluded until 1900 when the
Supreme Court of Pennsylvania finally upheld the
decision of the Court of Common Pleas of Luzerne
County in favor of the Catholics. (See Greek
Catholic Church v. Orthodox Greek Church, 46,
Atlantic Reporter: 72-77 [1900]. Most of the
Ruthenian priests that passed into Orthodoxy
eventually returned to the Catholic faith.

61. Rev. Hrushka returned to the Catholic faith in
1901.

62. Numerous articles by Ukrainian priests and laymen
in Svoboda, particularly during 1901-1902, re-
futing the Russian Orthodox Mission's claims,
assailing the immorality of their clergy, and
censuring "Moscophiles", illustrate the bitter-
ness of the struggle.

63. Uniia v Amerytsi, p. 20. The same figures are
given by the Russian Orthodox Kalendar Pravosl,
1901, cited by A. Levkov in Svoboda, April 11,
1901, p. 4.

64. According to Warne, Slav Invasion, p. 101-102,
the Presbyterians were the most energetic in
their missionary work among the Slavic immigrants at this time. The report of the Board of
Home Missions of the Presbyterian Church to the
Chairman of the Immigration Commission, dated
New York, November 22, 1910, illustrates the
extensiveness of the Presbyterian work among the
new immigrants, including the Ruthenians. See
U. S. Senate, Statements by Societies Interested
in Immigration, Reports of the Immigration Commission, Doc. No. 764, 61st Cong., 3d Sess.,
1911, XXIII, 297-301.

65. Shipman, "Immigration", p. 96-99.
66. Svoboda editorial, February 21, 1901, p. 2.
67. Ibid., September 19, 1901, p. 2.
68. See Uniia v. Amerytsi, pp. 35-44. On the other
hand, the Viestnik editorial, April 17, 1902, p.
4, indicated obvious satisfaction when it informed its readers that official notification of
Father Hodobay's appointment as Vicar for the
Ruthenian Catholics had been received. On May 8,
1902, pp. 1-2, the Viestnik contains an account
of the arrival and welcome of Hodobay and his

secretary Rev. John Korotnoky at Hoboken, New
Jersey, as well as a long biographical sketch of
the new Apostolic Visitor.

69. Cited by S. Gulovich, "Rusin Exarchate", p. 470.
Father Hodobay's letters to the Apostolic Delegate contain additional statistics concerning
the Ruthenian Catholics in America during 1904-
1905. It is interesting to note the great discrepancy between Hodobay's estimate of the number of Ruthenian Catholics in the different dioceses and those sent to the Apostolic Delegate by
the dioceses concerned. Based on his own observations, Hodobay believed that individual parishes submitted greatly reduced statistics in order
to keep down episcopal fees. See the specific
illustrations in Ambrose Senyshyn, "The East in
the West", The Ark III (May, 1948), 96-98.

70. Kalendar Sojedinenija, 1905, p. 160.

71. Viestnik, May 29, 1902, p. 2 which also summa-
rizes the agenda of the convocation.

72. Svoboda, August 7, 1902, p. 4.

73. See, for example, Viestnik, July 10, 1902, p. 1;
July 17, p. 2; July 24, p. 2; July 31, p. 2; etc.

74. Hanchin, "Istoria Sojedinenija", p. 46.

75. Rev. A. Pekar, OSBM, Our Past and Present: Historical Outlines of the Byzantine Ruthenian
Metropolitan Province (Pittsburgh, 1974), p. 40.

76. Hanchin, "Istoria Sojedinenija", p. 46.

77. The correspondence between Father Hodobay and the
Latin bishops provide clear illustrations of the
complexity of the jurisdictional problems faced
by Hodobay. For example: a misunderstanding
over an appointment of a priest to a Ruthenian
mission precipitated a series of strongly worded
letters between Hodobay and the Bishop of Erie,
Pennsylvania, as illustrated in Hodobay's letters
of June 24, August 1 and August 27, 1904, and by
the letter from the bishop, August 26, 1904; the
question of the transfer of church property was
the occasion of an extremely sharp letter from
the Bishop of Syracuse, August 30, 1904; while
the problem of married priests and their changing
parishes without permission of the bishop occa-
sioned a lecture-like letter from the chancellor
of the Archdiocese of Philadelphia (on the instructions of the Archbishop), November 12, 1904.
These letters, as well as others cited in the
following two footnotes, are in the archives of
the Ukrainian Archdiocese of Philadelphia.

78. Contributing further to the chaotic conditions

during Father Hodobay's period was the continued
arrival in greater numbers of married priests,
contrary to regulations, for whom Hodobay was
unable to obtain jurisdiction from the local
Latin Ordinaries. Some bishops, or their chan-
cellors, made specific requests that Hodobay not
recommend married priests to work in their diocese, stating that such priests would not be
admitted. For example: letter from the chancellor of the Archdiocese of Philadelphia, November
12, 1904, or the letter from the Bishop of
Cleveland, September 6, 1904. These priests,
however, carried on parish duties with only the
jurisdictions they obtained in Europe or with
none at all, thus greatly contributing to the
very unfavorable opinions that some Latin bishops
had of the Ruthenian priests. This is illustrated in correspondence such as the letter from the
Bishop of Erie, August 26, 1904, or that of the
Bishop of Syracuse, August 30, 1904.

79. In addition to his official responsibilities
relative to the Ruthenian Catholics, Father
Hodobay was also often involved in the problems
of other Eastern rite Catholic groups in America.
This is illustrated, for instance, by the following correspondence: Hodobay's letter to the
Archbishop of Boston, October 16, 1906, requesting jurisdiction for the Syrian rite Catholic
priest, Rev. Nananias Bouri, O.S.B.M.; letter
from Shaheen Haddad, November 1, 1906 (with
thirteen signatures), concerning an appeal by the
Syrian rite Catholic people of Boston for help in
obtaining a priest; Hodobay's reply, November 21,
1906, stating that he will submit the matter to
the Apostolic Delegate; Hodobay's letter to the
Apostolic Delegate, November 6, 1906, requesting
aid in the matter of obtaining the necessary
jurisdiction for Rev. Bouri, recently sent by the
Eastern Catholic Patriarch of Antioch and by the
Superior General of the Order of St. Basil the
Great for the Syrian rite mission in Lawrence and
Boston, Mass.

80. S. Gulovich, "The Rusin Exarchate", p. 474.

81. Letter to Cardinal Gotti, Prefect of the Sacred
Congregation of the Propagation of Faith to
Father Hodobay, dated March 8, 1907, advising him
that he is relieved of his duties as Apostolic
Visitor to Ruthenians in America. Amerykansky
Russky Kalendar, 1908, (Uzgorod, Hungary, 1907),
p. viii.

CHAPTER II

1. Walter Paska, <u>Sources of Particular Law for the</u>
   <u>Ukrainian Catholic Church in the United States</u>
   (Washington, D. C., 1975), p. 33, citing
   Sophronius Mudrij, OSBM, <u>De Transitu ad Alium</u>
   <u>Ritum</u> (Rome, 1973), pp. 102-103.
2. Rev. Leo I. Sembratovich, secretary of the Metropolitan during these years, provides us with a
   good general account of the role of the Metropolitan in influencing: 1) the Pope's decision to
   appoint a bishop, 2) the appointment of his candidate as most suited to end the chaotic conditions, 3) the acceptance of his candidate by the
   Austrian and Hungarian authorities interested in
   keeping the loyalty of their former subjects. It
   was particularly difficult to obtain the approval
   of the Hungarian government which feared that its
   former subjects, who made up the majority of the
   Ruthenian Catholics in the United States, might
   be swayed either towards Ukrainophilism or towards Moscophilism. See "Yak pryishlo do
   imenovania nashoho pershoho epyskopa v. Amerytsi",
   <u>Yuvyleiny almanakh Ukrainskoi Hreko-Katolytskoi</u>
   <u>Tserkvy u Zluchenykh Derzhavakh, 1884-1934</u> (Philadelphia, 1934), pp. 103-107.
3. A good biographical outline of Bishop Ortynsky's
   background can be seen in <u>America</u>, April 4, 1916,
   p. 2.
4. Full text in <u>Svoboda</u>, August 15, 1907, p. 4, and
   in the <u>Viestnik</u>, August 22, 1907, p. 4. All
   translations are by the writer.
5. The bishop's arrival and the official ceremonies
   held in his honor in New York on August 27th and
   28th, are reported in detail by both <u>Svoboda</u> and
   <u>Viestnik</u> in their respective issues of September
   5, 1907, p. 4.
6. St. Michael's was the first church to be blessed
   by a Ukrainian bishop in America. The bishop's
   day to day schedule from his arrival through
   October 29, outlined by the director of the Chancery, Rev. Vladimir Petrivsky, can be seen in the
   <u>Viestnik</u>, September 26, 1907, p. 4.
7. The bishop's official notice of his temporary address appeared in <u>Svoboda</u>, for the first time,
   September 5, 1907, p. 1, and in the <u>Viestnik</u> the
   same date, p. 4. In the absence of an official
   clerical Bulletin, the bishop's notices and
   regulations appeared in both papers. Ortynsky's
   long pastoral letter (<u>Poslaniie Pastirske Sotera</u>

Ortynskoho), of January 11, 1908, p. 9, also specifically refers to South Fork as his temporary
address upon his arrival in the United States.
The above letter henceforth referred to as
Poslaniie.
8. Svoboda, November 7, 1907, p. 1.
9. Literally hundreds of letters between Bishop
Ortynsky and the Apostolic Delegate in Washington,
numerous Latin bishops, and various other persons,
provide ample illustrations of these problems.
The writer will limit his references to those letters which have a direct bearing on the historical
development of the Ruthenian Church organization.
The letters are in the archives of the Ukrainian
Archdiocese of Philadelphia.
10. Acta Sanctae Sedis (Rome, 1908) XLI, 3-12 or AER,
XXXVII (VII), (November, 1907), 513-520. H. J.
Heuser's "The Appointment of a Greek Bishop in the
United States", pp. 457-466 of the same number
of the AER, contains a good discussion of the
principal provisions and regulations of this papal
letter. Acta Sanctae Sedis, hereafter cited as
ASS.
11. ASS., XLI, 4. Early in his administration Bishop
Ortynsky visited Latin bishops in whose territories numerous Ruthenians were domiciled (the
bishops of Altoona, Scranton, and Pittsburgh for
example) concerning the administration of the
Ruthenian Church. One of the important points
agreed upon was that no Ruthenian priest be given
jurisdiction within the territory of the Latin
ordinary without an understanding with Bishop
Ortynsky. See Viestnik, September 26, 1907, p. 4.
12. ASS., XLI, 7.
13. Ibid., p. 6.
14. See Svoboda editorial, November 21, 1907, p. 4.
15. Ibid., December 12, 1907, p. 4.
16. Hanchin, "Istoria Sojedinenija", p. 52. According
to Hanchin who was present at the welcoming banquet in New York for the new bishop, the President
of the Sojedinenije, in strong words, warned
Bishop Ortynsky that his organization and the people will never allow a policy intended to foster
Ukrainian partisan objectives. See also Svoboda,
September 5, 1907, p. 4.
17. Bishop Ortynsky in his Poslaniie of January 11,
1908, p. 15, made it clear that he did not know
about the papal letter until several weeks after
his arrival in the United States, when he was informed of it by the Apostolic Delegate. He con-

sidered the new regulations unjust to the
Ruthenian Church and its people, and immediately
protested against it.

18. The Galician "Moscophile" minority opposed Bishop
Ortynsky. _Svoboda_, September 26, 1907, p. 2,
lists the leading Moscophiles.

19. Ibid., December 26, 1907, p. 1.

20. Attacks on Ortynsky appeared in the _Viestnik_ immediately upon his arrival. For example: the
editorial on August 29, 1907, p. 4, represents a
relatively mild attack, whereas, on September 5,
p. 2, a very harsh attack was made where, among
other things, the bishop is accused of Latinization because he wore a "Polish Velum." On the
other hand, _Svoboda_, September 19, 1907, p. 4,
contains an early and strong indictment of the
Transcarpathians for these attacks on the bishop,
and the Galicians in general. It should be made
clear that not all of the Transcarpathian priests
were opposed to Bishop Ortynsky, nor did they en-
dorse attacks on him. Those opposed to Ortynsky,
like Revs. Cornelius Lavrisin, Nicholas and
Gabriel Chopey, Nicholas Jackovich, Alexander
Dzubay, Alexis Holosnyay and others, were mostly
from Munkacs and traditionally strongly Magyarized in their outlook. (Hanchin, "Istoria
Soyedinenija" pp. 53-54). There were also Transcarpathian priests that backed Ortynsky, such as,
Revs. Gorzo, Hanulya, Mirossay, V. Balogh,
Goidics, and Volensky. (_Viestnik_, December 15,
1910, p. 5) Rev. V. Balogh, for example, in a
letter to the _Svoboda_ entitled "Amer. Russkomu
Viestnikovi do vidomosti" protested strongly
against _Viestnik's_ (September 5, 1907, p. 2)
attack on Bishop Ortynsky "in the name of the
Transcarpathian priests and people", and requested that the "editors retract articles which
insulted our bishop". (See _Svoboda_, September
26, 1907, p. 4.)

21. The literature explaining the fight against
Bishop Ortynsky continues to be polemic. In the
Kalendar Sojedinenija, 1942, p. 47, for example,
one may read that ". . . because of his
Ukrainophil policy and latinization a 'struggle'
began, which continued until his death in 1916.
. ." The statement is an oversimplification of
the problems involved. Rev. Stephen C. Gulovich,
on the other hand, in his excellent article suggests that Bishop Ortynsky had two strikes
against him before he set forth on any policy.

"As for the Rusins", Gulovich writes, "who by
this time could boast of a commanding majority,
Bishop Ortynsky was guilty of an 'unpardonable
crime': he came of Ukrainian stock!" (See
Gulovich, "The Rusin Exarchate", p. 475) The
Poslaniie of January 11, 1908, referred to above,
provides a clear picture of Bishop Ortynsky's
interpretation of the early struggle against him.

22. The bishop's official announcements appeared in
Svoboda, October 2, 1907, p. 1, under the titles:
"Do vidomosty vsim hr. -kat sviashchenykam
Spoluchenykh Derzhav Pivnichnoi Ameryky" and "Do
vidomosty vsim deliegatam hr.-kat. hromad
tserkovnykh v Spoluchenykh Derzhavakh". The
announcements also appeared in Viestnik, October
3, 1907, p. 4.

23. Svoboda, October 2, 1907, p. 1.

24. Viestnik, October 3, 1907, p. 4.

25. Official report of the priests' assembly from the
bishop's Chancery, Svoboda, November 7, 1907,
p. 3.

26. Ibid., the report, dated from Philadelphia on
October 26, 1906, and signed by the bishop's
secretary Rev. Vladimir Petrivsky, details the
proceedings and decisions of the assembly.

27. The bishop's official announcement, Svoboda,
October 2, 1907, p. 1.

28. The parish delegates conference was actually held
at Arlington Hall, St. Marks Place, New York
City.

29. Official report of the parish delegates assembly
from the bishop's Chancery, dated from Philadelphia on October 26, 1907, Svoboda, November 7,
1907, p. 3.

30. Ortynsky's official four page announcement to his
priests, (Vsechestneishym oo. dukhovnim do
vedomosty i zaistosovania), of October 1, 1912,
clearly indicates, as an illustration, that all
churches were not yet properly signed over to the
bishop, that many churches were not paying the
cathedraticum, and that some priests were leaving
or accepting parishes without the bishop's approval.

31. Ortynsky's Poslaniie, January 11, 1908, p. 19-20.

32. A series of letters by the Bishop of Altoona to
Bishop Ortynsky, for instance those dated May 4,
1908; July 5, 1908; September 10, 1908; and March
27, 1911, illustrate the jurisdictional difficulties faced by the two bishops and the amicable
attempts to solve them. Conversely, a series of

letters from the Bishop of Trenton to Ortynsky,
for example those dated March 30, 1911, June 18,
1912; March 12, 1913; and March 24, 1913, as well
as Bishop Ortynsky's draft (undated) in reply to
the above mentioned letter of March 30, 1911, and
his draft of March 19, 1913, in reply to the letter of March 12, 1913,referred to above, illustrate the extremely strained relations that sometimes developed as a result of the intolerable
conditions of divided jurisdiction. The above
letters, as well as those referred to in the following footnote, are in the archives of the
Ukrainian Archdiocese of Philadelphia.

33. The transfer of Ruthenian Church property from
the corporation of a Latin rite bishop to a legal
corporation of Bishop Ortynsky was often a long
drawn out process requiring the attention of the
bishops involved, the Apostolic Delegate, and of
course of legal counsels. In the case of the
transfer of property located in the territory of
the Trenton Diocese, Ortynsky's attorney corresponded frequently with the bishop regarding the
progress of the Bill of Incorporation for the
Ruthenian Church in the State of New Jersey, as
illustrated by his letters, dated between January
28, 1913 and May 8, 1914. Similarly the two
bishops involved in this transfer as well as the
Apostolic Delegate corresponded with one another,
sometimes in strong language, as shown by the
letters of the Bishop of Trenton, dated February
27, 1913, and of Bishop Ortynsky, dated March 20,
1913 to the Apostolic Delegate, and by the letters of the Delegate to Ortynsky, dated May 2,
1913 and December 18, 1914.

34. The Official Catholic Directory, 1908, (Milwaukee),
p. 153. From 1912 the Directory has been published in New York. Hereafter cited as CD.

35. Ibid., 1909, p. 153.

36. See Propamiatna knyha ukrainskoi katolytskoi
katedry, 1942 (Philadelphia), pp. 11-17, which
contains several informative recollections by
early immigrants concerning the organization of
the first two Ruthenian churches in Philadelphia,
their internal conflicts, and the establishment
of the present cathedral by Bishop Ortynsky.
Pages 33-34 list the pastors and curates of the
cathedral to 1942. Hereafter cited as Knyha
katedry. See also, Peter Isaiv, "Istoriia
katedralnoi parokhii", Shlakh (Philadelphia),
November 26, 1950, pp. 10-14, for a useful

summary of the history of the Ukrainian cathedral, written on the occasion of the fortieth anniversary of its blessing. The entire Ukrainian section of this issue of the diocesan newspaper is devoted to the history of the cathedral.

37. The Catholic News (New York), October 22, 1910, p. 8. This is an extremely valuable report, almost the entire newspaper page, containing every conceivable detail connected with the Consecration ceremonies, including the names of many of the participating Latin and Ruthenian clergy, and other dignitaries. (Cardinal Vincenzo Vannutelli was the Papal Legate to the Eucharistic Congress in Montreal.)

38. Ibid., p. 8.

39. Grodsky, "Vidvidyny Ameryky Mytr. A. Sheptytskym v 1910 rotsi." Kalendar Provydinia, 1927, p. 104. This is a very valuable first hand report of the Metropolitan's visit to the United States and Canada by the Metropolitan's secretary who accompanied him on the entire four month tour.

40. See the report on Sheptytsky's arrival in the New York Times, August 24, 1910, p. 6.

41. Viestnik, December 15, 1910, p. 4.

42. "Priests Charges Denied," Public Ledger (Philadelphia), December 2, 1910, p. 2.

43. Within the year, for example, on August 31, 1911, 46 priests, the vast majority of whom originated from Transcarpathia, signed a long complaint addressed to the Pope, which contained a bitter attack on Bishop Ortynsky. The letter was in the possession of the late Very Rev. John D. Taptich, Wilkes-Barre, Pa.

44. Grodsky, "Vidvidyny Ameryky," pp. 112-117.

45. Metropolitan Sheptytsky's discussions proved fruitful for it was mainly on his recommendations that, on October 13, 1912, Pope Pius X nominated Rev. Nykyta Budka as the first Ukrainian bishop in Canada.

46. For a good summary of the history and accomplishments of the Sisters of St. Basil (from Galicia) in the United States see America (Philadelphia), September 28, 1961. The entire issue is dedicated to the Sisters of St. Basil on the occasion of their Fiftieth Anniversary in America.

47. Eparkhiialny Vistnyk, II (December 20, 1915), 10. This is the official Diocesan Bulletin for the clergy founded by Bishop Ortynsky in 1914. Hereafter cited as Visty.

48. See Visty, II, 10-12, for a detailed list of the

orphanage properties, the yearly cost of operation, and the financial burden sustained by the bishop since the founding of the orphanage in 1911, through October 1915.

49. Zachary Orun, "Misionarska shkola im. Sv. Apostola Pavla v Filadelfii", _Kalendar Provydinia_, 1918, p. 235. Father Orun was the Director of the boys from 1917 until his death in 1918.

50. ASS., XLI, 6.

51. In addition to the seminary, and orphanage, and a vocational school were to be erected at the Yorktown site. See _Svoboda_, August 18, 1910, p. 1.

52. Letter to Bishop Ortynsky from the Imperial and Royal Austro-Hungarian Consulate in Philadelphia, No. 53, June 26, 1915. Cited by Willibald M. Ploechl, "The Slav-Byzantine Seminary in Washington, D. C." ECQ, VI (October-December, 1946), 490. Ploechl, who was visiting professor of Oriental Canon Law at Catholic University, had first hand contacts with Bishop Bohachevsky, the Ukrainian Seminary in Washington, and its students who attended the University.

53. Draft of Bishop Ortynsky's reply to the Austro-Hungarian Consulate in Philadelphia. n.d. Cited by Ploechl, Ibid., p. 490.

54. Joseph Dzendzera, "Ukrainski bohoslovy v dukhovnim semynary v Boltymor," _Kalendar Provydinia_, 1918, p. 237. Rev. Dzendzera was the Director of the seminarians from 1918.

55. Peter Poniatishin, "Ukrainska Tserkva i U. N. Soyuz", _Propamiatna khyha Ukrainskoho Narodnoho Soyuza, 1894-1934_ (Jersey City, 1936), p. 290.

56. Poniatishin, "Z moikh spomyniv," _Ukraintsi u vilnomu sviti: yuvileina knyha Ukrainskoho Narodnoho Soyuza, 1894-1954_ (Jersey City, n.d.), p. 35. Rev. Poniatishin was a delegate to this convention.

57. _Svoboda_, November 10, 1910, p. 1, contains the official explanation by the officers of the Soyuz for not putting into effect the change in the name of the organization.

58. Anton Tsurkovsky, "Desiatlitny yuvyley Provydinia", _Kalendar Provydinia_, 1924, p. 2. Tsurkovsky was editor of _America_ from 1914 and later the Recording Secretary of the Providence Association.

59. _America_ was first published in 1912 at Hartford, and then in New Britain, Connecticut, by a press owned by Revs. R. Zalitach, A. Pavliak, V.

Dovhovich and others. For a summary of the history of this paper see the fifty-year jubilee edition of <u>America</u>, October 25, 1961.

60. Tsurkovsky, "Desiatlitny yuvyley," pp. 8-9.
61. Ibid., p. 4.
62. Letter of Apostolic Delegate, Archbishop Bonzano, dated August 25, 1913, notifying the American clergy of the Vatican's decision, <u>AER</u>, XLIX (October, 1913), 473-474.
63. On May 26, 1963, Metropolitan Ambrose Senyshyn opened the Fiftieth Jubilee Year, with a Mass of Thanksgiving in the Cathedral of the Immaculate Conception in Philadelphia, honoring the fiftieth anniversary of the establishment of the first Byzantine-Slavic rite exarchy in the United States.
64. Healy, "Our Catholic Ruthenians", <u>AER</u>, XCIII (July, 1935), 79.
65. Philadelphia and its immediate vicinity contained five churches or chapels at this time. Besides the Cathedral of the Immaculate Conception on North Franklin Street and the Holy Ghost parish at Passyunk Avenue, there were the chapels at the Convent of St. Basil the Great on Franklin Street, St. Michael's at 9th and Buttonwood, and SS. Peter and Paul on Penn Street, Clifton Heights. (See <u>CD</u>. 1914, p. 819.)
66. Ibid., p. 823.
67. It is interesting to note that Cleveland was the only other city, beside Philadelphia, which contained five congregations at this time. All are listed as parishes. (See <u>CD</u>., 1914, p. 823.)
68. Ibid., pp. 818-823.
69. Ibid., p. 823.
70. Visty, I (April 28, 1914), 1.
71. CD., 1914, p. 819.
72. <u>Visty</u>, I (April 28, 1914), 1. Pages 1-3 contain a detailed list of the officials of the new diocese.
73. Ibid., I (May 22, 1914), 1.
74. Shortly before Ortynsky left for Rome the Transcarpathian priests had again requested that Ortynsky aid them to obtain a bishop from Transcarpathia.
75. <u>Acta Apostolicae Sedis</u>, (Rome, 1914), VI., 458-463, or <u>AER</u>, LI (November, 1914, 586-592). <u>Acta Apostolicae Sedis</u> hereafter cited as <u>AAS</u>.
76. <u>AAS</u>., VI, 462.
77. Ibid., p. 463.
78. Ibid.

79. Foraneus, "Some Thoughts on the Ruthenian Question in the United States and Canada", AER, LII (January, 1915), 42-50, also "The Ruthenian Question Again", AER, LII (June, 1915), 645-653.
80. Donald Attwater, The Christian Churches of the East (Milwaukee, 1948), I, 19.
81. Svoboda, October 10, 1907, p. 1.
82. Ibid., April 21, 1910, pp. 2, 3, and 6, continued in subsequent issues.
83. See below, pp. 40-41.
84. Pravoslavnyi russko-amerikaskii kalendar, 1915, (New York, 1914), p. 119.
85. Archbishop Evdokim's letter, dated February 24, 1916, appeared in the Viestnik on July 28, 1916, pp. 4-5, four months after Ortynsky's death. The letter is also cited in Svoboda, August 8, 1916, p. 3.
86. Bishop Ortynsky's pastoral letter dated October 8, 1914, cited by Sochockyj, "Ukrainska tserkva", p. 226.
87. Thousands of dollars, as well as quantities of medical supplies, and gift packages were sent to help reduce the plight of Ruthenian war victims. See, for instance, the bishop's notices in Visty, II (May 24, 1915), 3, Ibid., III, (March 8, 1916), 9-10.
88. The growing Ukrainian national consciousness among the immigrants from Austrian Galicia was part of the reason for the opposition to Bishop Ortynsky by the Magyarized and Russophile immigrants from Hungary.
89. Svoboda, April 1, 1916, p. 2. Also America, April 3, 1916, p. 2. A very interesting little pamphlet entitled Zhytie, smert i pokhorony S.S. Ortynskoho, (Scranton, Pa., 1916), p. 8 (unnumbered), indicated that in addition to the Ruthenian and the Latin rite clergy and a Syro-Maronite (Antiochene rite) bishop, there were also Presbyterian, Methodist, and Episcopalian ministers, a Jewish Rabbi, and an Orthodox priest present at the funeral. (p. 12) The pamphlet contains some excellent photographs of the funeral procession and the throngs outside the cathedral.
90. Svoboda, April 1, 1916, p. 2, also America, April 3, 1916, p. 2.
91. See above, p. 24.
92. CD., 1916, p. 789.

CHAPTER III

1. CD., 1916, p. 782.
2. Nine Magyar congregations later associated themselves with Rev. Poniatishin's administration.
   Since Poniatishin did not speak Hungarian, he
   administered them by appointing as their Dean
   Rev. Victor Kovalytsky, the Hungarian priest from
   Perth Amboy, New Jersey, who spoke both Ukrainian
   and Hungarian. (See Father Poniatishin's "Iz
   chasiv administratsii eparkhii", Almanakh Tserkvy,
   p. 111). Rev. Poniatishin's various recollections are extremely valuable to the history of
   the Ukrainian Catholics in the next eight and one
   half years. We will frequently rely on them in
   this chapter which deals exclusively with the
   administration of Father Poniatishin.
3. Ibid., p. 111.
4. Visty., III (May 17, 1916), 4.
5. Svoboda, April 15, 1916, p. 2, contains a good
   biographical sketch of its former director and
   the newly appointed administrator.
6. Ibid., October 24, 1916, p. 2.
7. Ibid. Resolution five was deemed necessary since
   some of the leadership of the Federation of
   Ukrainians espoused socialist and anti-clerical
   views.
8. Ibid.
9. Poniatishin, "Spohad iz chasiv syritstva Ukr.
   Kat. Eparkhii v Amerytsi", Knyha katedry, p. 46.
10. U. S. Bureau of the Census, Religious Bodies:
    1926, II (1929), 514. This official government
    report, which presents 213 different denomina-
    tions in America, fails to list the relatively
    numerous Byzantine rite Catholic churches under
    any category whatsoever. The only reference to
    their existence that this writer found in the
    voluminous report was on pp. 512-513 where the
    point is made that in the more recent immigration,
    large numbers have come to the Russian Orthodox
    Church from the old Austria-Hungary, "who be-
    longed to what are known as the Uniate churches."
11. Poniatishin, "Iz chasiv", p. 111.
12. Ibid.
13. Ibid.
14. New York, Laws of New York (1917), II, c. 353,
    1155-1159.
15. Poniatishin, "Iz chasiv", p. 111.
16. The problem of secession to Orthodoxy also led to
    bitter conflicts among the Transcarpathians at
    this time. See for example, Viestnik, August 3,

10, and 17, 1916, p. 1.

17. Poniatishin, "Iz chasiv", p. 111.

18. Father Dzubay was also known by the name of Stephen; however, official sources like the diocesan Visty and also the Catholic Directory use the name Alexander. For useful background on Father Dzubay becoming an Orthodox bishop see America, August 11, 12, 16, 19, and 24, 1916, p. 2. Later Dzubay repented and returned to the Catholic Church, living in seclusion in St. Paul's Friary, Graymoor, New York.

19. The term "cantor" needs additional explanation for the reader not familiar with the Byzantine Slavic rite. A cantor is a layman trained to lead the congregation in responses to the priests prayers in the Liturgy and in other religious services. In the Byzantine rite the responses are often involved; consequently, whenever possible each parish hires a cantor who, because of his training and position in the parish, often has considerable influence among the parishioners.

20. Poniatishin, "Iz chasiv", p. 112.

21. See, e.g., Poniatishin's letter dated September 30, 1916, published in Catholic News, October 7, 1916, and reproduced in Svoboda, October 28, 1916, p. 3.

22. Poniatishin, "Spohad", pp. 48-49.

23. Poniatishin, Iz chasiv", p. 112.

24. In his letter of September 15, 1922, to Rev. Paul Procko, the pastor in Altoona, Poniatishin suggests that the priest organize a parish in Uniontown, Pa., which is located over 100 miles southwest of Altoona. In another letter dated March 12, 1923, to Father Procko, then in New Kensington, Pa., Poniatishin suggests that he hold services in neighboring Vandergrift and Leechburg. In Leechburg, according to Poniatishin's information, there were fifty Ukrainian families which had completely fallen under Bolshevik influence and who would possibly return to their faith with the help of a priest. The above letters, as well as the letter referred to in the following footnote, are in the possession of the writer.

25. Official form letter from Poniatishin to the priests under his administration, dated December 5, 1923, announcing the "Missionary Fund" regulations.

26. Temporary Diocesan Statutes of the Byzantine Rite Apostolic Exarchy of Philadelphia, (Philadelphia,

144

1953), I, 9.
27. Visty, I (October 8, 1914), 2.
28. Dzendzera, "Ukrainski bohoslovy", p. 237.
29. See Msgr. James Mooney's letter from Seton Hall
    College to Father Poniatishin, dated April 5,
    1918, and also Poniatishin's undated draft to
    Msgr. Mooney in reply to the above letter. Both
    letters are in the archives of the Ukrainian
    Archdiocese of Philadelphia.
30. Poniatishin, "Iz chasiv", pp. 113-114.
31. Ibid., p. 112.
32. Ibid.
33. Orun, "Misionarska shkola", p. 236.
34. Ibid.
35. Visty., I (October 8, 1914), 4.
36. Poniatishin, "Spohad", p. 49.
37. Poniatishin, "Iz chasiv", p. 112.
38. Visty., II (May 24, 1915), 1.
39. Poniatishin, "Iz chasiv", p. 112.
40. Ibid.
41. A letter from a law office in Pittsburgh to
    Father Poniatishin, dated May 9, 1922 (thus late
    in his administration) illustrates the dificul-
    ties still experienced in placing building con-
    tracts because of the title being in Bishop
    Ortynsky's name. The letter is in the archives
    of the Ukrainian Archdiocese of Philadelphia.
42. For example, in his letter to the newly appointed
    pastor in New Kensington, Pa., dated Newark, N.J.,
    December 28, 1922, Poniatishin points out that
    the high Cathedraticum debt of the pastor's new
    church represents at least partial arrears in
    payment during the entire period of Poniatishin's
    administration, since the death of the bishop in
    1916. Letter in the possession of the writer.
43. See above, pp. 34.
44. See above, p. 39, resolution #5.
45. The official letter, dated November 2, 1916, de-
    claring the withdrawal of the Soyuz from the
    Federation was published in Svoboda, the organ of
    Soyuz, on November 7, 1916, p. 2. A detailed
    explanation for the withdrawal is found in Ibid.,
    December 16, 1916, p. 2.
46. Zhoda Bratstv (Compact of Brotherhoods), was an-
    other organization of American Ukrainians orga-
    nized in Olyphant, Pennsylvania, in 1913.
47. The official notification of the organization of
    the Alliance on November 1, 1916, published in
    Svoboda, December 5, 1916, p. 1.
48. Poniatishin, "Ukrainska Tserkva", p. 293.

49. A letter from a Second Assistant Secretary in the State Department to Poniatishin, chairman of the Ukrainian National Committee, dated December 16, 1918 (in reply to Father Poniatishin's letter of November 18, 1918) indicates that the State Department was glad to utilize the committee as a medium through which to acquire information regarding the Ukraine, but that it was not prepared to recognize it as an official spokesman of the Ukrainian people. Letter in the archives of the Ukrainian National Museum in Chicago.

50. Protocol from the first general convention, America, December 30, 1916, p. 3.

51. Rev. Poniatishin discussed in detail the steps leading to the proclamation of the Ukrainian Day immediately after the events themselves in "Istoriia ukrainskoho dnia", Svoboda, March 31, April 3, 1917, p. 3. Many years later he again wrote about these events in "Ukrainska sprava v Amerytsi", Yuvileiny Almanakh Svobody, 1893-1953 (Jersey City, 1953), pp. 66-71. (Hereafter cited as Almanakh Svobody.) Both accounts are alike in substance.

52. Congressman Hamill in his remarks in the House, on February 21, 1917, reviews the specific contacts with Father Poniatishin which brought to his attention the humanitarian objectives of the Ukrainians. See U. S., Congressional Record, 64th Cong., 2d Sess., 1917, LIV, Part 6 (Appendix part 1-5), 522.

53. U. S., Congressional Record, 64th Cong., 2d Sess., 1917, LIV, Part 3, 2751-2752.

54. Ibid., Part 4, 3909.

55. U. S., Statutes at Large, XL, part 2, 1645-1646.

56. According to Father Poniatishin, the American Ukrainians are indebted to Congressman Hamill, President Wilson's secretary Tumulty, attorney Kearns, and a half-dozen other Senators and Congressmen, who understood their aspirations and through whose influence the Ukrainian Day became a reality. See Svoboda, April 3, 1917, p. 3, and "Ukrainska sprava", p. 76.

57. "Ukrainska sprava", p. 76.

58. Copy of Father Poniatishin's letter to Congressman James A. Hamill, dated December 27, 1916. Letter in the archives of the Ukrainian Museum in Chicago.

59. Poniatishin, "Ukrainska sprava", p. 71.

60. Ibid., p. 73.

61. U. S., Congressional Record, 65th Cong., 3d Sess.,

1918, LVII, Part I, 434.
62. The following examples illustrate the significant role of Father Poniatishin and of his committee in their attempts to bring aid to the Ukrainian people in Galicia. In a letter to the Executive Committee of the National Catholic War Council, in Washington, D. C., dated October 30, 1919, Poniatishin pointed out that Metropolitan Sheptytsky, the Primate of Galicia, was interned by the Polish authorities, that about 200 of his priests were held in the notorious Brigitta prison (Brygidky, the building of the former monastery of St. Brigitta) in Lviv, that relief work had not penetrated into Galicia, and again requested an investigation of conditions and aid for the Ukrainians in East Galicia. In a five page memorandum to the United States Secretary of State, dated September 7, 1920, Poniatishin vigorously complained about Polish atrocities against Ukrainian Catholics in Eastern Galicia, such as, the closing of three theological seminaries, internment of bishops, and the shooting of eleven priests, and begged the United States to use her influence to put an end to these conditions. Finally a letter from the Department of Foreign Affairs of the Western Ukrainian Republic in exile, dated from Vienna, November 10, 1921, and signed by Gregory Myketey, officially thanked Poniatishin for taking the first politico-diplomatic action to inform the United States government and President Wilson about the Ukrainian viewpoint concerning Galicia. The above letters are in the archives of the Ukrainian Museum in Chicago.
63. Poniatishin, "Ukrainska Tserkva", p. 294.
64. Ibid., p. 299.
65. Ibid.
66. For the immediate concerns and objectives of the United Ukrainian Organizations see e.g., America, October 30, p. 2; November 15, p. 1; December 5, p. 1; December 8, p. 3; December 11, 13 and 15, p. 1; and December 27, 1922, p. 2.
67. Poniatishin, "Ukrainska Tserkva", p. 297.
68. Sheptytsky's letter to Poniatishin, dated from Lviv, Galicia, December 18, 1920, in the archives of the Ukrainian Museum in Chicago.
69. Poniatishin, "Z moikh spomyniv", pp. 21-22.
70. Metropolitan's letter to Poniatishin, dated from Philadelphia, January 30, 1922, in the archives of the Ukrainian Museum in Chicago.

71. Poniatishin, "Z moikh spomyniv", p. 28.
72. Ibid.
73. Ibid., p. 30.
74. Ibid., p. 27.
75. America, March 15 and 20, 1922, p. 1.
76. Ibid., August 11, 1922, p. 1.
77. Sheptytsky's letter to Poniatishin dated from Chicago, October 29, 1922, in the archives of the Ukrainian Museum in Chicago.
78. Address by Myshuga in Newark, N. J., November 18, 1945. Excerpts cited by Poniatishin, "Z moikh spomyniv", pp. 32-33.
79. See Sheptytsky's letters to Poniatishin dated October 18 and 29, 1922, and his undated letter from Philadelphia during the 1921-1922 Christmas Season. The letters are in the archives of the Ukrainian Museum in Chicago.
80. America, September 12, 1922, p. 2, lists the names of all the clerics attending the retreat.
81. Ibid., September 11, 1922, p. 1.
82. For a report on the official farewell festivities held on November 7, 9 and 10 in honor of Metropolitan Sheptytsky, see America, November 15, 1922, p. a.
83. November 15, 1922, p. 2.
84. The Transcarpathians were particularly interested in obtaining their own bishop. For example; on May 11, 1916, seventy-four priests originating from Hungary met and petitioned for a bishop of their own. (See Viestnik, August 10, 1916, p. 1.) In a reply to a cablegram from the Sojedinije, Bishop Anthony Papp of Munkacs, Hungary, notified the President of the Sojedinenije by a letter dated February 10, 1924, that within three months a bishop would be appointed for the Transcarpathians. (See Viestnik, August 7, 1924, p. 8.) Finally, Rev. Constantine S. Roskovich, the spiritual director of the Sojedinenije, in his report at the 18th Convention of that organization stated that as a result of many discussions and letters with Metropolitan Sheptytsky and the chancery of Cardinal Hayes of New York, and with their help, the wishes of the Transcarpathians for their own bishop were about to be realized. (See Protokol XVIII Konvencii Sojedinenija Greko Kaftolioeskich Russkich Bratstv, 1924, (Homestead, Pa.), p. 14. Also in Viestnik, July 17, 1924, p. 5.

CHAPTER IV
1. CD., 1925, p. 759.
2. Ibid., p. 754.
3. In 1945, Bishop Kotsylovsky, whose diocese of Peremyshl was situated within the borders of Poland, was arrested and transferred to Soviet Ukraine where he died a prisoner in 1947.
4. Viestnik, August 21, 1924, p. 1. Also Svoboda, August 16, 1924.
5. Ibid.
6. With the arrival of Bishops Takach and Bohachevsky Fathers Martyak and Poniatishin, administrators of the diocese since the death of Bishop Ortynsky in 1916, returned to their respective parish duties.
7. Eparkhilialni Visty (Philadelphia), V (October, 1924, 2. Hereafter cited as Visty.
8. Originally Bishop Ortynsky founded the Eparkhiialny Vistnyk in 1914; however, after his death it was discontinued until it was reestablished, on a larger scale, by Bishop Bohachevsky in October 1924, as the Eparkhiialni Visty. This is a most important primary source for the history of the Ukrainian Catholic Church in America. Since the formation of the Archdiocese in 1958 it is called the Arkhieparkhiialni Visti.
9. Visty, V (November, 1924), 5.
10. Ibid., p. 6.
11. Ibid.
12. Ibid., pp. 7-8.
13. Ibid., V (April, 1925), 6.
14. Ibid., VI (February, 1936), 10.
15. Ibid., VI (October, 1925), 2-3.
16. Ibid., V (October, 1924), 4.
17. Ibid., VII (November, 1926), 5.
18. Ibid., VII (May, 1927), 1.
19. Ibid., p. 2.
20. Ibid., V (October, 1924), 2.
21. Undoubtedly the Archbishop's glowing report of the political and religious developments in the Ukraine since the Soviet government came to power contributed to this support. Teodorovich's views are extensively reported in Svoboda, February 19, 1924, page 3, by a representative of that paper who interviewed him. The essence of the Archbishop's opinions is as follows: 1) the Ukrainian Soviet government was bringing about complete Ukrainianization; 2) the Ukrainian Autocephalous Orthodox Church, which is controlled by the people themselves, has become the spokesman

of the Ukrainian national movement; 3) at the present time the most important goal was to organize within the Ukrainian Autocephalous Church all those who, as a result of the internal church fights, are now without the benefit of religious solace. Obviously Teodorovich's strongly democratic and patriotic sentiments would impress the politically disturbed Ukrainian patriots in exile. Incidentally, the Archbishop's name is given as "Khvedorovich" rather than the commonly used "Teodorovich."

22. Simon Demydchuk, "Naslidky ukrainskoho derzhavnytstva na ridnykh zemliakh", Piatdesiatlittia Ukrainskoi Katolytskoi Tserkvy sv. Yura, 1905-1955 (New York, n.d.), p. 75. Hereafter cited as Tserkva sv. Yura. Demydchuk was a Ukrainian war exile from Europe who became an important participant in Ukrainian affairs in America.

23. The leaders of the opposition, for example, claimed that within a year eighteen churches fell away from the exarchy and that more than twenty thousand changed their faith. See the official call for action by the opposition to Bishop Bohachevsky in Svoboda, December 3, 1926, p. 3.

24. Official notice signed by the leaders of the opposition dated from Philadelphia, November 29, 1926, Ibid.

25. The "Recollections of Joseph Krupka", 1959 (MS in the files of the Ukrainian Archdiocese of Philadelphia), contain very interesting illustrations of specific events and persons participating in this struggle. Krupka, an eyewitness of these events in the mid-west, credits Dr. Osyp Nazaruk for convincing the large Ukrainian communities in Hamtramck, Detroit, and Chicago to remain loyal to the bishop by his lecture in Hamtramck in the Fall of 1925 (pp. 10-20). He also credits the "Hetmantsi" of the Sich organization with generous support of the Church and Bishop Bohachevsky in this conflict. (p. 20). The support of the bishop by the Sich is attested to, e.g., by the letter of Dr. Stephen Hrynevetsky, the chief officer of that organization, dated from Chicago, December 14, 1926, which included a substantial contribution toward the seminary and future high school, and by the bishop's acknowledgment. See Visty, VII, (January, 1927), 3-5. The bishop's links with the "Hetmantsi", supporters of Hetman Paul Skoropadsky's claims to rule independent

Ukraine, tended to alienate from him the opponents of Skoropadsky.

26. _Visty_, VI, (November, 1926), 5.
27. Ibid., (January, 1927), pp. 5-6.
28. Protocol of the Congress, _Svoboda_, January 11, 1927, p. 4.
29. For the discussions and the decisions of the congress, see the Protocol of the Congress, Ibid., January 8, 1927, p. 5, and January 10, 11, and 12, 1927, p. 4.
30. _Visty_, VI (November, 1926), 5; VII, (January, 1927), 10; VII, (April, 1927), 8, etc.
31. The bishop's regulation dated January 6, 1927. See _Visty_, VII, (January, 1927), 6-7.
32. See the Protocol of the Congress in _Svoboda_, January 10, 1927, p. 4 for the charges made by the opposition and the matters which they considered most important.
33. _Visty_, VII, (March, 1927), 1-2; and (April 1927), pp. 2-4. At the same time the bishop charged that the leaders of the opposition "in return for the ruin of Holy Church and rebellion against her lawful authority - promise a Ukraine, and rebellion and ruin they call patriotism." See Ibid., (April, 1927), p. 4.
34. See, for instance, Andrew Khlystun, "V spravi konkordatu Polshchi z Rymom," _America_, September 5, and 10, 1925, p. 2, in support of the Concordat, and the editorial in _Svoboda_, March 23, 1925, p. 2, in opposition to it.
35. Letter of the Very Rev. Theodorovich, O.S.B.M., September 9, 1932, cited by Bishop Bohachevsky, "Dopovnenniia do vasyliianskoi litopysy," _Kovcheh_, III (December, 1948), 147. The bishop's article translated into English, is also printed in the English edition of this monthly. See _The Ark_, III (October-November, 1948), 184-188, 193, 195-196. A useful, although not entirely accurate, summary of the establishment of the Basilian Fathers in the United States is provided by Rev. Vladmur Gavlich, O.S.B.M., "Vasyliiany u Zluchenykh Derzhavakh Ameryky" _Pamiatka Novoi Provintsii oo. Vasyliian_ (New York, 1948), pp. 18-22.
36. _AER_, LXXXI (August, 1929), 167-176.
37. The translation of articles cited is that of the canonist Rev. V. Pospishil, _Interritual Canon Law_, p. 207.
38. Ibid., p. 207.
39. Ibid., p. 208.

40. Ibid., p. 209.
41. Ibid.
42. In a relatively short period of time twenty-six
    congregations separated themselves from the ex-
    archy. See Poniatishin's article in _Tserkva sv.
    Yura_, p. 144.
43. Paul Procko, "Pochatky i rozvytok ukrainskoho
    semynaria y Zluchenykh Derzhavakh," _Propamiatna
    knyha ukrainskoho katolytskoho kaledzha, 1940_,
    (Philadelphia, p. 23. Hereafter cited as _Knyha
    kaledzha_. Father Procko was Rector of the ex-
    archy's seminary from 1926 to 1941.
44. _Visty_, VI (December, 1925), 5-6; Ibid., (November,
    1925), p. 6, lists the students in the Phila-
    delphia seminary for 1925-26, and the seminar-
    ians in Rome.
45. Father Procko, "Pochatky i rozvytok", p. 23, list
    the following seminarians who were sent from
    Philadelphia to Rome and who later returned to
    the exarchy as priests: Revs. Stephen Chehansky,
    Dr. Basil Fedish, Dr. Stephen Knapp, Michael
    Bobersky, Leo Pelensky, Michael Skorodynsky,
    Joseph Schmondiuk (subsequent Metropolitan of
    Philadelphia), John Babiak, and Dr. Stephen
    Hrynuch.
46. _Visty_, VI (September, 1925), 6.
47. A day school was opened by the Sisters in Phila-
    delphia, in 1916; however, with the death of
    Bishop Ortynsky the school, which had no finan-
    cial support except that provided by the bishop,
    was forced to close.
48. _America_, September 10, 1925, p. 1. The new
    school was solemnly blessed on November 29, by
    Bishop Bohachevsky. See Ibid., December 1, 1925,
    p. 1.
49. _Visty_, VIII (February, 1933), 10.
50. Ibid., (May, 1933), p. 19.
51. _America_, August 29, 1933, p. 1.
52. Ibid., September 7, 1933, p. 1; September 9,
    1933, p. 2.
53. _Visty_, IX, (September, 1934), 63.
54. Ibid., (November, 1934), p. 63.
55. Ibid., (September, 1934), p. 63.
56. Ibid., X (August, 1935), 34.
57. Ibid., VIII (May, 1933), 23.
58. Ibid., (June, 1933), p. 35.
59. Ibid., X (November, 1935), 44.
60. Ibid., p. 45.
61. See e.g., Osyp Nazaruk's article in _Kalendar
    syritskoho domu_, 1926, p. 67.

62.   *America*, September 19, 1933, p. 2.

CHAPTER V

1.   Heally, "Our Catholic Ruthenians", AER, XCIII
      (July, 1935), 78-79.
2.   An Encyclical Letter of Pope Pius XI on the East-
      ern Churches. A translation of Rerum Oriential-
      ium (Washington, D. C. n.d.), p. 8.
3.   Schmal, "The Ruthenian Question in the United
      States," AER, XCVIII (November, 1937), 456. Al-
      though this article is dated, the writer recom-
      mends it highly.
4.   The reader should be aware that celibacy is a law
      which does not bind all the priests of the Cath-
      olic Church. The majority of the secular priests
      of the Oriental Church were married men. The
      introduction of the celibacy rule among the
      Byzantine-Slavic priests in the United States was
      the result of pressure on the Vatican by the
      Latin rite bishops.
5.   Visty, XI (November, 1936), 69.
6.   Ibid., XV (August, 1940), 34; November, 1940, p.
      47. For a list of all the schools operated by
      the Basilian Sisters and Sister Servants in
      1940, as well as for the statistical information
      concerning these schools, see Knyha kaledzha, p.
      51.
7.   Visty, XII (May, 1937), 16; XIII (August, 1938),
      30; (November, 1938), pp. 42-43, pp. 51-53.
8.   Ibid., XVI (November, 1941), 43-44.
9.   Ibid., p. 44..
10.   St. Michael's Ukrainian Greek Catholic Church of
      Woonsocket, R. I. v. Bohachevsky, 196, Atlantic
      Reporter, pp. 796-812 (1938).
11.   Visty, XIII (November, 1938), 43-44.
12.   Ibid., XIV (May, 1939), 28-29.
13.   Ibid., p. 29. The Pittsburgh Deanery remained
      vacant temporarily. (See CD., 1940, p. 639).
14.   Ibid., XIII (November, 1938), 42.
15.   Connecticut, Special Laws (1939), XXIII, Part 1,
      300.
16.   The bishop's announcement dated March 5, 1941, in
      Visty, XVI (May, 1941), 16.
17.   Ibid., p. 16.
18.   Visty, XV (February, 1940), 3.
19.   Ibid., XVI (November, 1941), 42-43.
20.   Ibid., XV (May, 1940), 14.
21.   Ibid., XVII (August, 1942), 24.

22. Ibid., p. 24, contains an authoratative brief biographical sketch of Bishop Senyshyn.
23. For a detailed account of the consecration ceremonies see Shlakh, October 31, 1942, p. 1.
24. America, October 17, 1940, p. 2
25. Visty, XV (May, 1940), 20.
26. Ibid., XX (August, 1945), 38.
27. CD., 1945, p. 779.
28. Ukraine: A Concise Encyclopaedia, I (Toronto, 1963), 911. David Martin, "Not 'Displaced Persons' - But Refugees", The Ukrainian Quarterly, IV (Spring, 1948), 109-114, estimates that perhaps up to five million Ukrainians were scattered through western and central Europe at the end of the war. The great majority of these were repatriated, voluntarily or forcibly, to the USSR.
29. The Apostolic Delegate's letter thanking Bishop Bohachevsky for his letter and check is reprinted in Visty, XXI, (February, 1946), 2.
30. Bishop Senyshyn's address, November 13, 1952, at the annual bishop's meeting in Washington, D. C. See The Ark, VII, 145.
31. Bohdan Karpovich, "Pomich bratovi z dalekoi dorohy" Tserkva sv. Yura, p. 184.
32. During the period under discussion, Bishop Senyshyn celebrated the Pontifical Mass at special Catholic observances in the following major cities: New York, Chicago, Buffalo, Boston, Washington, Philadelphia, Milwaukee, Baltimore, Albany, Newark, Wilmington, St. Paul, Rochester, and Syracuse.
33. Of special interest to this study were a series of articles concerning the development of the Ukrainian Catholic Church in the U.S. entitled "The East in the West" which appeared in The Ark, a monthly publication founded by Bishop Senyshyn and devoted primarily to Byzantine-Slavic ecclesiastical and cultural affairs. The first of these articles appeared in Vol. II (Jan., 1947), 11-12, 18. Six of the others follow in the same volume. Another substantial article, useful for this study, was "The Ukrainian Catholics in the United States," Eastern Churches Quarterly, VI (October-December, 1946), 439-457.
34. In the early 1960's the organization was renamed the League of Ukrainian Catholics. At an interview in Philadelphia, August 6, 1964, Metropolitan Senyshyn indicated his interest in this association by expressing the hope that a local chapter of the league be formed in every parish

of the archeparchy.

35. During the writer's interview on August 6, 1964, Metropolitan Senyshyn stated that about eighty-five per cent of the current Ukrainian seminarians were formerly members of Altar Boys Societies. Obviously, the Metropolitan regarded this society important to the Ukrainian Catholic Church in America.

36. For background on Ukrainian Redemptorist Fathers see Michael Hrynchyshyn, C.SS.R., "Redemptorists of the Ruthenian Rite," Jubilee Book of Redemptorist Fathers of the Eastern Rite (Yorktown, Canada, 1955), pp. 375-422.

37. See The Way, December 19, 1942, pp. 8-9 for background on the Sisters of St. Francis of Assisi.

38. Visty, XXIII (February, 1948), 10. See also Franciscan Fathers, "History of the Commissariat of the Byzantine Rite", The Ark, III (June-July, 1948), 116-121.

39. Decree from the general headquarters of the Basilian Order of St. Josaphat in Rome, dated July 23, 1948, and signed by Rev. Hlib Kinakh, O.S.B.M., Vicar General; and by Rev. Joseph Zaiackhivsky, O.S.B.M., General Secretary, in Pamiatka novoi provintsii oo Vasyliian (New York, 1948), p. 7. Very Rev. Nickolas Kohut, O.S.B.M., became the first Superior General of the new province. He was succeeded, shortly thereafter, by Very Rev. Maxim Markiw, O.S.B.M.

40. Solemn Blessing and Dedication of St. Basil's Home, 1954, pp. 27-28, the official brochure published on the occasion of the blessing of the new orphanage.

41. Mention must also be made of the College of the Basilian Fathers in Glen Cove, L. I., New York, which the Basilians conducted for their own seminarians.

42. Visty, XXIII (November, 1948), 65.

43. Ibid., XXIV (February, 1949), 8.

44. Ibid. (November, 1949), p. 76.

45. Visty, XXVII (August, 1952), 78. Volumes VII of The Ark and of Kovcheh (June-July, 1952) are dedicated to a comprehensive report, including numerous photographs, of the impressive dedication ceremonies.

46. AAS., XLI, 1949, 89-119.

47. Ibid., XLII, 1950, 5-120.

48. Ibid., XLIV, 1952, 15-150.

49. Ibid., p. 144.

50. Ibid., XLIX, 1957, 433-600.

51. _Visty_, XXIV (May, 1949), 41.
52. Ibid., p. 33.
53. Ibid., XXVI (August, 1951), 73-74.
54. Ibid., (November, 1951), p. 114.
55. See, for example, _Visty_, XXVII (May, 1952). This issue is replete with specific regulations to the clergy of the exarchy.
56. Ibid., (May, 1952), p. 51.
57. Ibid., (February, 1952), pp. 19-24.
58. Ibid., (May, 1952), p. 49.
59. Ibid. (February, 1952), p. 25. It is interesting to note that it was in this post-war period of expansion that, for the first time, a priest of the Ukrainian exarchy in America was named an Apostolic Prothonotary, with the title of Rt. Rev. Monsignor. The priest so honored by the Vatican, May 16, 1948, was the Vicar General of the exarchy, Very Rev. Anthony Lotowytz. See _APS._, XXXXI (1949), 302.
60. Ibid., XXVI (May, 1951), 45.
61. _Temporary Diocesan Statutes of the Byzantine Rite Apostolic Exarchy of Philadelphia_ (Philadelphia, 1953).
62. _Visty_, XXVIII (November, 1953), 89.
63. Ibid., XXV (February, 1950), 10.
64. Ibid., XXVI (February, 1951), p. 9.
65. See above, pp. 73-74.
66. Interview with Metropolitan Senyshyn, Philadelphia, August 6, 1964.
67. The arrival of displaced priests from Europe appears to have reached its peak in 1950, based on the official notices of new jurisdictions received which appeared in the _Visty_.
68. S. O. Pidhainy, I. I. Sandul and A. P. Stepovy, eds., _The Black Deeds of the Kremlin_, Vol. I, Book of Testimonies (Toronto, 1953), 511-527, contains useful information relating to these matters.
69. _The Catholic Standard and Times_ (Philadelphia), February 15, 1963, pp. 1, 3, and 4 contains a biographical sketch of Metropolitan Slipyj, as well as a summary of the vicissitudes of the Ukrainian Catholic Church in Europe since World War II. After his arrival at the Vatican, where he now resides, Metropolitan Slipyj was appointed to the Second Vatican Council's Commission for the Eastern Churches, and in late 1963 he was named a member of the Sacred Congregation for the Eastern Churches. On January 25, 1965, he was elevated to the dignity of Cardinal by Pope Paul

VI, thus becoming the fourth Ukrainian prelate in history to be so honored.

70. ASS., XXXXV (1953), 522. The title of Right Rev. Monsignor was bestowed upon Msgr. Stock in 1968. Many view the bestowal by Rome of western ecclesiastical titles upon Eastern rite clerics as an obvious illustration of the continued latinization of the Eastern rite Catholics.
71. Ibid., XXXXVI (1954), 294.
72. National Eucharistic Marian Congress of the Oriental Rites (1954), a 36 page program brochure of the Congress, contains a very impressive list of the members of the Latin and Oriental rites hierarchy and clergy participating in the Congress.
73. AAS., XXXXIX (1957), 116-118, contains the Apostolic Constitution Optatissimo unitatis, dated July 20, 1956, dividing the Philadelphia exarchy and creating the new exarchy in Stamford
74. See the announcement of the creation of the new diocese and the appointment of its first bishop in the official diocesan paper, The Way, August 19, 1956, p. 1.
75. CD., 1957, p. 726.
76. The Way, October 21, 1956, p. 13.
77. Ibid., p. 9.
78. CD., 1957, p. 719.
79. The Way, August 19, 1956, p. 1. A total of sixteen parishes and missions comprising the new deanery is listed in Visty, XXXI (November, 1956), 101.
80. Visty, XXXI (November, 1956), 101.
81. Ibid., p. 100.
82. The Way, November 4, 1956, pp. 9-10 contains the most useful of several biographical sketches of the new bishop-elect.
83. See Ibid., November 18, 1956, pp. 9-10 for an account of the consecration ceremonies.
84. Visty, XXXI (November, 1956), 101-102.
85. Ibid., XXXII (November, 1957), 74.
86. Two months earlier in May, the Vatican had honored three additional priests of Archbishop Bohachevsky's exarchy as Papal Chamberlains, with the title of Very Rev. Monsignors. The priests so honored were Rev. Leo Adamiak, Stephen Chehansky, and Jaroslav Gabro. See AAS., L (1958), 754.
87. AAS., LI (1959), 156-157.
88. Papal bull of July 10, 1958, appears in Ukrainska Mytropolia, pp. 45-46. (Also in Shlakh, November

1, 1958, p. 2.

89. Ibid., pp. 55-56.
90. See The Way, November 12, 1956, p. 1-2, for a detailed account of the installation ceremonies.
91. Canon 422 of the motu proprio Cleri Sanctitati of June, 1957, orders every diocese to hold a convocation at least every ten years. See ASS, XLIX (1957), 558.
92. The secretary's report of the consultors meeting Shlakh, April 30, 1958, p. 4.
93. Visty, XXXIV, (May, 1959), 40.
94. Ibid., (August, 1959), p. 64. The letter also lists the appointed officials for the convocation.
95. Statutes of the Archeparchy of Philadelphia (Philadelphia, 1960), pp. VII-XVIII.
96. AAS., LII (1960), 849.
97. Ibid., LIII (1961), 285.
98. The Way, January 18, 1961, p. 3. See the fine brief biography of Archbishop Bohachevsky recently written by his brother Dr. Daniel Bohachevsky, Vladyka Konstantyn Bohachevsky, Philadelphia, 1980.
99. Shlakh, January 25, 1961, p. 3-4.
100. On September 12, 1968, the remains of Metropolitan Bohachevsky and Bishop Ortynsky were transferred from the old cathedral to a crypt located below a side altar of a newly erected cathedral.
101. Shlakh, January 18, 1961, p. 4. See also Visty, XXXVI (February, 1961), 2.
102. Shlakh, August 23, 1961, p. 1. The Papal bull of July 14, 1961, naming Bishop Senyshyn as the new Metropolitan appears in Ibid., November 15, 1961, p. 2.
103. AAS., LIV (1962), 493-495.
104. Shlakh, December 6, 1961, p. 2, contains a map directory of the new diocese, as well as the boundaries of the Archeparchy of Philadelphia and of the Stamford Diocese.
105. Ibid., October 18, 1961, p. 1, contains the most informative of several short biographical sketches of Bishop Gabro.
106. Ibid., November 1, 1961, p. 1, 7. The consecration of Bishop Gabro and Bishop Augustine Hornyak, O.S.B.M., Exarch for the Ukrainian Catholics in England and Wales, was the first dual consecration of Ukrainian Catholic bishops in the United States.
107. Shlakh, December 27, 1961, pp. 1-3.

108. Directory, Byzantine Rite Ecclesiastical Province of Philadelphia (Philadelphia, 1962), p. 218. (Hereafter cited as Ukrainian Directory.)
109. Shlakh, January 17, 1962, pp. 1, 3.
110. The Way, January 31, 1962, pp. 1, 4.
111. Ibid., pp. 1, 4.
112. AAS., LIV (1962), 749. The title of Right Rev. Monsignor was bestowed upon Msgr. Paska on September 7, 1963. (See AAS., LVI (1964), 841.)
113. Ukrainian Directory, 1962, p. 124.
114. See The Way, November 1, 1961, pp. 1, 7. The occasion was graced by the attendance of five Archbishops, 24 bishops, civil officials, and numerous clergy and faithful.
115. AAS., LIV (1962), 539.
116. The Way, February 21, 1962, p. 4.
117. The Way, January 17, 1962, pp. 1-2. The Way, January 17, 1962, pp. 1-2. The writer also learned about some of the specific plans concerning the proposed new cathedral in an interview with Metropolitan Senyshyn in Philadelphia on May 7, 1962.

CHAPTER VI

1. The difficulties faced by bishops Ortynsky and Bohachevsky during their episcopate's were discussed in chapters two and four above.
2. One In Christ, (London), I, no. 4 (1965), 395-396. For the original Latin version see AAS., LVII (1965), 76-89. Two early commentaries on the decree were written by scholars from the Ukrainian Archeparchy: Rev. Meletius Woinar, O.S.B.M., "Decree on the Oriental Catholic Church," The Jurist, XXV (April, 1965), 173-255; and Msgr. Victor J. Pospishil, Orientarium ecclesiarum; the decree on the Eastern Catholic Churches of the II Council of Vatican, canonical, pastoral commentary (New York, 1965).
3. Critical, nevertheless informative, publications concerning the eastern policies of the Vatican include: Ulisse A. Floridi, Mosca A Il Vaticano (Milan, 1976); Hansjakob Stehle, Die Ostpolitik Des Vaticans, 1917-1976 (Munchen-Zurich, 1975); Thomas E. Bird and Eva Piddubchesen, eds. Archiepiscopal and Patriarchal Autonomy (New York, 1972); "The Vatican's Ostpolitic", Newsweek (December 6, 1971); "The Vatican's

Ostpolitic", <u>Newsweek</u> (December 6, 1971); Eva Piddubchesen, <u>And Bless Thine Inheritance</u> (New York, 1970).

4. Msgr. Basil Shereghy, <u>The Way</u>, November 14, 1976, p. 3.

5. For the critical views expressed by several of the spokesmen of the protestors, see e.g. <u>The Evening Bulletin</u> (Philadelphia), December 8, 1969, p. 4; <u>Philadelphia Inquirer</u>, of the same date; <u>The Catholic Standard and Times</u>, December 11, 1969, p. 9.

6. <u>Kryza-Crisis</u> (New York), March 21, 1971, p. 1. This is the first issue of a small newspaper published by members of the Student Ad-Hoc Committee for a Self Governing Ukrainian Catholic Church.

7. For additional details concerning the consecration ceremonies of bishops Stock and Losten, as well as brief biographies of the two auxiliaries, see <u>The Way</u>, June 6, 1971, pp. 1 and 2.

8. See, e.g., reports of the impassioned addresses made by Ukrainian prelates at the World Synod of Bishops in Rome, <u>The Sunday Bulletin</u> (Philadelphia), October 24, 1971, Sec. one, p. 5. A similar account appears in the <u>Philadelphia Inquirer</u> of the same date. See also Edward B. Fiske's reports from Rome to <u>New York Times</u>, November 1, 1971, p. 13. Fiske's follow-up report appeared on November 2.

9. As an illustration, see the comprehensive letter to Pope Paul VI from the Society for the Patriarchal System, Philadelphia, April 18, 1973 in <u>Diakonia</u> (New York), IX, no. 3. (1974), 294-300.

10. Stephen Skrobach, "Nevzhe zh tse pravelny shliakh", <u>Amerika</u>, December 30, 1970, quoted in <u>Shlakh</u>, January 17, 1971, p. 4.

11. The entire program planned for the Ukrainian participation in the 41st International Eucharistic Congress in Philadelphia is outlined in <u>The Way</u>, May 2, 1976, p. 3. Bishop Losten's formal expression of gratitude to those contributing to the success of the Ukrainian program appears in <u>Shlakh</u> September 12, 1976, pp. 1-2.

12. See <u>The Way</u>, October 3, 1976, p. 1 for a list of the hierarchy co-celebrating the Liturgy on September 16.

13. <u>The Way</u>, October 10, 1976, p. 3.

14. See <u>Shlakh</u>, October 10, 1976, p. 2.

15. Ibid., November 7, 1976, p. 2.

16. See above, pp. 73-75, 80-81.
17. See Shepherd in Chains (Philadelphia, 1962).
18. Visty, XLIX (November 1974), 44-45.
19. For a list of cities and towns where new churches were built see Shlakh, November 30, 1975.
20. AAS., Vol. LXV, no. 4 (April 1973), 223; and Vol. LXVII, no. 8 (August 1975), 507.
21. Visty, LI (May-August 1976), 36.
22. The American Ukrainian Catholics have traditionally provided spiritual and material aid to the Ukrainian communities in Europe, South America and elsewhere. Father Theodore Weneck, O.F.M. from the Franciscan Monastery in Sybertsville, Pa., for instance, is currently on assignment in Argentina's Chaco and Formosa Provinces. In 1970, when earthquakes caused severe damages and resulted in extreme hardships in Yugoslavia, Metropolitan Senyshyn sent more than $12,000.00 to Archbishop Gabriel Bukatko, administrator of the Ukrainian Catholic Church in Yugoslavia, to help relieve the sufferings of his people. See Visty, XLV (May, 1970), 34.
23. The Way, March 28, 1976, p. 1.
24. Ibid., November 20, 1977, p. 4, contains informative details of the extent of the restoration as well as of the original construction of the cathedral. The ceremonial blessing of the restored historic church by Bishop Gabro took place on October 30, 1977 in the presence of Cardinal Cody of Chicago, seventeen Eastern and Latin rite bishops, over 30 priests, Chicago's mayor Michael J. Bilandic and some 1200 of the faithful. See, e.g., Shlakh, December 4, 1977, pp. 2-3.
25. The Way, June 13, 1976, p. 1.
26. Shlakh, January 29, 1978, p. 2.
27. The Way, October 31, 1976, p. 1.
28. For a list of the co-celebrants of the Liturgy, as well as of other dignitaries attending the installation ceremonies, see Shlakh, December 18, 1977, pp. 1 and 3.
29. For a list of the co-celebrants, as well as of other dignitaries attending the colorful ceremonies, see Shlakh, January 8, 1978, p. 1.
30. For a complete list of participants in the funeral ceremonies for Archbishop Schmondiuk see the formal expression of thanks by the chancellor of the Philadelphia Archeparchy, Msgr. Robert Moskal's "Podiaka," Shlakh, January, 1979, p. 1.
31. See, e.g. "Ukrainians Protest Selection of

Bishop," _Philadelphia Inquirer_, Sept. 27, 1979, p. 3-B.; Ibid., "Protest on Naming of Bishop Disputed," Sept. 28, 1979, p. 9-A.; "Pope's Nominee Criticized," _Philadelphia Bulletin_, September 27, 1979; "Appointment Stirs Ukrainian Community," _Catholic Standard and Times_, October 4, 1979, p. 15.

32. See Paula Herbut, "Ukrainian Cardinal Backs Pick of Philadelphia Church Head," _Philadelphia Bulletin_, Nov. 3, 1979.

33. Including the present writer.

34. See Dale Mezzacappa, "Harmony Theme for Pope's Visit with Ukrainians," _Philadelphia Inquirer_, Oct. 5, 1979, p. 5-a.

35. See Rev. Ronald Popivchak's account of the ceremonies in _The Way_, Dec. 2, 1979, p. 1.

36. See Rev. Popivchak's account in _The Way_, December 30, 1979, p. 1.

37. See _Shlakh_, October 7, 1979, p. 2 for a concise biographical sketch of Archbishop-elect Lubachivsky.

38. "Yednist ukrainskoi katolytskoi iyerarkhii" _Shlakh_, November 4, 1979, p. 2.

39. For copies of the Pope's letter in Latin, its English translation, and other related materials see _Ukrainian Vatican Synod 1980: A Documentary_ (Stamford, Ct., 1980). English translation of the letter also in _The Way_, April 13, 1980, p. 3.

40. See Peter Hebblethwaite, "Pope Calls Ukrainians to Secretly Planned Synod," _National Catholic Reporter_, March 28, 1980, p. 7, for critical analysis of the timing of the announcement, six days prior to the event.

41. See below, p. 107.

42. Jerry Filteau, "Pope Seeks Unity at Ukrainian Synod," _Catholic Standard and Times_, March 27, 27, 1980, p. 2.

43. _Svoboda_ editorial, April 1, 1980, p. 2; Cardinal Slipyj's opening address at the Synod, _Shlakh_, April 11, 80, p. 1; Victor J. Pospishil's "'Pomisnist' Achieved: Ukrainian Catholic Church Receives Equality with Eastern Catholic Patriarchates," _Ukrainian Vatican Synod 1980: A Documentary_, p. 15-24 (np.).

44. See "Leader of Ukrainian Catholics" in _New York Times_, March 28, 1980, p. A12. For Ukrainian translations of the Papal bulls naming Lubachivsky coadjutor of Cardinal Slipyj and another naming him administrator of the Philadelphia See, which became vacant when he was

named coadjutor, see <u>Shlakh</u>, June 15, 1980, p. 1.
45.   See Peter Hebblethwaite, "Ukrainian Synod Picks
      Lubachivsky," <u>National Catholic Reporter</u>, April
      11, 1980, p. 28.
46.   See <u>Nova Zoria</u>, April 6, 1980, pp. 1 and 9, for a
      detailed account of the several funeral ceremon-
      ies. <u>Nova Zoria</u> is the official newspaper of the
      Ukrainian diocese in Chicago.
47.   Rev. John Bilanych of Christ the King parish in
      Philadelphia, was named Vicar General, and admin-
      istered the archeparchy in Lubachivsky's absence.
48.   See <u>Shlakh</u>, March 8, 1981, p. 1 for details of
      the consecration ceremonies.
49.   See <u>Shlakh</u>, April 21, 1981, pp. 1 and 7 for the
      names of the distinguished participants, and
      other details of the installation and banquet
      that followed.
50.   See <u>The Way</u>, February 8, 1981, p. 1-2 for most
      complete of several brief biographical sketches
      of the new Metropolitan.
51.   Archbishop Lubachivsky departed for Rome on April
      28, 1981 to take up his new duties as coadjutor
      and successor to Cardinal Slipyj, the head of the
      Ukrainian Catholic Church. See <u>Sklakh</u>, May 10,
      1981, pp. 7-8 for Lubachivsky's own summary of
      his life's journey which he outlined at the fare-
      well banquet in his honor in Philadelphia on
      April 23.
52.   See <u>The Way</u>, February 8, 1981, p. 1 for a concise
      biographical sketch, one of several brief biog-
      raphies of the new bishop.
53.   On August 14, 1981, it was announced that Amer-
      ican born Monsignor Robert M. Moskal, chancellor
      of the Philadelphia Archeparchy, was named an
      auxiliary bishop to Metropolitan Sulyk by Pope
      John Paul II. The appointment is the result of
      the proposals by the Ukrainian bishop's first
      regular synod held in November-December, 1980.
      Bishop-designate Moskal was consecrated on Octo-
      ber 13, 1981 at the Cathedral of the Immaculate
      Conception in Philadelphia. For brief biogra-
      phies of Bishop Moskal see <u>Svoboda</u>, August 19,
      1981, p. 1, or <u>The Way/Shlakh</u>, August 23, 1981,
      p. 1.
54.   <u>The Way</u>, March 22, 1981, pp. 1 and 2. See also
      Metropolitan Sulyk's address delivered at the
      banquet following his installation in Phil-
      adelphia for possible stop-gap measures to al-
      leviate the serious problem of shortage of
      priests. <u>The Way</u>, April 12, 1981, pp. 2, 3, and

7. The same address in Ukrainian is in <u>Shlakh</u>, April 19, 1981, pp. 4 and 6.

CONCLUDING REMARKS

1. There are presently separate jurisdictions in America for the Ukrainians, Transcarpathians (Byzantine Ruthenian Metropolitan Province), Maronites, Melkites, and Armenians. On July 17, 1981 Pope John Paul II established an Exarchate for the Armenians in the United States and Canada, with New York City as its See.
2. "Reflections on the Eastern Tradition," <u>One in Christ</u>, VII (1971), 358.
3. "Theology, Pluralism and the American Experience," <u>Diakonia</u> XI (1976), 72.

INDEX